# THE WARLORDS

## Hindenburg and Ludendorff

# THE WARLORDS

## Hindenburg and Ludendorff

John Lee

WEIDENFELD & NICOLSON

*To my friend*

*and fellow biographer,*

*my wife, Celia*

First published in Great Britain in 2005
by Weidenfeld & Nicolson.

10 9 8 7 6 5 4 3 2

© John Lee, 2005

A CIP catalogue record for this book is available from the British Library.

ISBN 0-297-84675-2

Printed in Great Britain by
Butler & Tanner

Weidenfeld & Nicolson
The Orion Publishing Group Ltd
Orion House, 5 Upper Saint Martin's Lane, London, WC2H 9EA

www.orionbooks.co.uk

# Contents

# Map list

*chapter one*

# The Prussian Military System

It might, at first, seem crude to label the military leaders of a twenti-eth-century European nation, with an elected parliament, as 'warlords'. This is surely a term one would normally apply to ancient or medieval societies, or to the lawless 'failed' states of more recent times. The origins of modern Germany were so completely determined by its armed forces that the foundations were laid for an unusual relationship between the army and society. The war that Germany entered into in 1914, and which should have ended in swift and decisive victory, produced such a crisis in every aspect of the nation's life that it opened the way for the army leaders to assume an unprecedented level of lead-ership. Perhaps unwillingly, they found themselves heading a coalition of industrial, financial and political forces almost permanently at log-gerheads with the official government of the state and, ironically, their emperor.

Initially the emperor, his government, the elected Reichstag and the people were united in a bid to defeat what they perceived to be a coalition of enemies bent on humiliating Germany and denying her a proper place in the world. After the dream of a quick victory rapidly faded, the press delivered up to the people some much needed heroes in the persons of Field Marshal Paul von Hindenburg and General

Erich Ludendorff, the 'saviours' of East Prussia from the Russian menace. These men hoped to consolidate their success and settle the war in the East quickly and decisively. Instead they found themselves locked in dispute with the chief of the General Staff (Erich von Falkenhayn) who still saw the defeat of the French and British on the Western Front as the main task at hand. When he did decide to make a major effort in the east, he carefully excluded Hindenburg and Ludendorff from the principal role.

As Falkenhayn's strategy failed to deliver any of Germany's foes to the peace table, and the blockade of Germany put intolerable strains on her economy and people, Hindenburg and Ludendorff were summoned by their emperor to assume the supreme command of the German armies in the field. Under their leadership the Great General Staff gradually spread its influence over the entire economy, the press, and ultimately parliament itself. They waged war on government ministers of whom they disapproved and inserted candidates of their choice. They imposed new economic programmes that marshalled the desperately straitened resources of the nation and brought them to a peak of readiness for one last try at winning the war by purely military means. Working from their army headquarters through a network of sympathetic military colleagues and right-wing political and economic forces, theirs was truly a 'silent dictatorship'. Their great love for their country and its remarkable armed forces would see them lead both to within a whisper of victory and to complete ruin.

Hindenburg and Ludendorff were archetypal products of perhaps the most professional army in the history of the world. They were formed by a military system that had grown up out of dire necessity. By looking at the evolution of this system we can begin to understand just how remarkable was their achievement.

How had Germany come to such a position, where she found herself facing a seemingly overwhelming coalition of enemies in the first total industrial war? How to explain that, outnumbered from the start and increasingly so, she could come so close to winning the war in 1918 despite her near exhaustion?

The collection of kingdoms, principalities, dukedoms, free cities and petty states, spiritual and temporal, that we know as Germany (a unified country only since 1871) is and was peculiarly vulnerable in terms of its military geography. The great North German Plain was a natural path for invaders from the East, debouching from Western Russia and Poland. To the west was one of the first and most powerful of nation states, France; to the north a warlike Sweden; to the south and east the puissant majesty of the Austrian Empire. The so-called Holy Roman Empire was all the organisation Germany could boast of and it was a battleground for other and mightier powers. The ravages of the Thirty Years' War, with its absolute drop in population numbers as war and disease held sway in middle Europe, was perhaps the nadir of German fortunes.

Germans, by whatever name they called themselves, were obliged to pay attention to their defences and, if they were known at all as soldiers, it was not as particularly special ones. Their *ritters* might teach some cavalry techniques in the sixteenth century; their *landsknechts* copied the famous Swiss pikemen and provided much mercenary employment for German warriors. But it was the Spanish *tercios*, or the standing army of France, or even the red-coated British who were the more famous as soldiers before the eighteenth century.

Germans are not genetically different from their European neighbours. They are not naturally better fighters, or from particularly militaristic societies. They have had their share of humiliations in battle, with the twin defeats of Jena and Auerstadt in 1806 bringing them to a low that was a profound shock to the heirs of Frederick the Great's Prussia. The poor reputation of 'German' troops in the Federal armies of the American Civil War continues to modify any idea we may have of the German as a 'superior' fighting man.

Something must have taken root in Prussia that was to turn a

Prussian-led Germany into the military phenomenon it has undoubtedly been in the nineteenth and twentieth centuries. The accession of Frederick William as the Hohenzollern Elector of Brandenburg in 1640 marked the start of something new. Frederick William was to leave his mark as the Great Elector for his role in transforming the fortunes of this backwater state. He was, quite simply, a man who had had enough. Being an able administrator, he built up a small, compact, efficient and well-trained army whose very existence prevented his bellicose neighbours from treating the indefensible territory of Brandenburg-Prussia as the doormat of north-eastern Germany. By 1688 he had created a thriving economy, with an excellent tax base; had tamed the Prussian Junkers and tied their fortunes to the military service of the state and could field an army of 30,000 men who commanded respect from all about them. Their victory over Swedish forces at the battle of Fehrbellin in 1675 marked their arrival on the historical stage as a force to be reckoned with.

His successor, Elector Frederick III, ruled from 1688 to 1713 and judiciously secured the improvements made by his father. By supporting the Holy Roman Emperor Leopold in his claim to the Spanish throne, he achieved royal status in 1701, but only as 'King in Prussia'. Prussian contingents served in the armies of Marlborough and Eugene and impressed all who saw them with their steady character. Frederick William I, king from 1713 to 1740, was the man who radically altered the balance of power in northern Europe. His obsession with all things military, combined with a shrewd ability to avoid embroilment in other people's wars, led to a massive increase in the power of the state. His efficient bureaucracy could cut royal expenditure and double overall income; his extravagance over the 'giants' recruited to the Potsdam Grenadiers should take nothing away from the excellence of the drill instilled in his army, which was a model of what could be achieved with eighteenth-century technology. He bequeathed to his successor an army of 83,000 disciplined men and a war chest containing the fabulous sum of seven million thalers.

How he must have regretted the fact that his son was despised as a flute playing, effeminate, philosophising boy. How astounded he would have been to see Frederick II declare himself king of Prussia, and promptly fling his army at the Austrian Empire and seize the province of Silesia in a series of brutal battles. In the Seven Years' War Frederick the Great showed himself to be a genius in war but he fought the magnificent Prussian Army to the point of destruction and, despite achieving astonishing victories and surviving terrible defeats, was on the point of being utterly overwhelmed by numerous enemies when, by a stroke of luck, Russia passed into the hands of one of his greatest admirers, Tsar Peter III, who made peace and withdrew from the coalition ranged against him.

The army of Frederick the Great was admired by all Europe and widely imitated. Like many victorious armies, it rested on its laurels and paid the price by being utterly destroyed by a vigorous new power in one of Napoleon's finest campaigns in 1806–7. The army of Frederick the Great was not the model for subsequent German success. Instead, in the aftermath of defeat, a happy circumstance brought together a remarkable group of men who not only recreated the Prussian Army and led it to victory but who started a process that led to a prime role for the army in the reunification of Germany and, ironically, to its eventual destruction.

Gerhard Scharnhorst (1755–1813), the son of a Hanoverian farmer, was so obviously talented a young man that he rose quickly in the Hanoverian Army, and was singled out and invited to join the Prussian artillery, being ennobled in 1802. He was soon transforming the military education of young officers, and running a military discussion society for officers at Berlin, where Karl von Clausewitz came to his attention. He saw the defeat of 1806 as inevitable, was made a prisoner after von Blücher's fighting retreat to Lübeck, and was released in an exchange of officer prisoners. Thus he was able to fight on into 1807 as chief of staff to Lestocq's Prussian corps supporting the Russians. His excellent service at the battle of Eylau and the siege of Königsberg brought him to the notice of King Frederick William III.

The king made him head of the Military Reorganisation Committee after the humiliation of the Peace of Tilsit in July 1807. He had the support there, against several reactionary old generals, of Prime Minister vom Stein and the able Colonel August von Gneisenau, both coincidentally, also of non-Prussian origin. The bringing together of three such men was fortuitous – the bookish but unprepossessing Scharnhorst, the intensely patriotic Stein and the intellectual warrior hero Gneisenau. When the terms of the harsh Treaty of Paris (1808) limited Prussia to an army of 42,000 officers and men, all long-service volunteers with no national militia or reserves allowed, Scharnhorst's plans for national conscription were frustrated. He did manage to remove older conservative officers from his Committee and recruit excellent young reformers: Karl von Grolman, Hermann von Boyen and Karl von Clausewitz. Together with Gneisenau, they made a formidable intellectual team, able to analyse problems and conceptualise solutions and reforms. All were able to prove themselves in the field from 1812 to 1815.

The obvious failures of command and control in 1806 made the staff system a prime candidate for reform. That the reformers had themselves all been so competent in this field made them the right men for the task. Scharnhorst's own humble origins helped the claims of non-noble citizens for officer advancement. They were able first to insist on the improvement of uniforms, service conditions and pay scales to drag the Prussian Army into the nineteenth century.

But these fine intellects also studied military history deeply and recognised that armies were dynamic organisations, where changing with the times was not merely necessary but vital. Success under one rule could so easily become decay under a less talented successor (a coded reference to Prussia's own recent past). Unless, that is, the factors essential for continuing success could be institutionalised into the very fabric of the army, and ideally into the state itself, which needed a new relationship with its ruler and its army. These military reformers were clearly seeing the larger picture, taking in the whole of society in their bid for modernity and success. Good practice, perhaps even best practice, would become so completely embedded in the organisation and the system as to survive any and all changes in personnel and circumstance. They consciously set out to create a military system that would survive and prosper regardless of external factors. Scharnhorst quite specifically stated that the problem would often be poor quality Prussian generals (he dare not specify that they were often royal and invariably aristocratic) and that the new breed of specially trained General Staff officers would be needed to support their commanders, 'providing the talents that might otherwise be wanting among leaders and commanders'.

The liberal reformers favoured a mass people's army, based on a patriotic citizenry that felt it had a stake in the society, organised by an enlightened and efficient disciplinary code. It would be a career open to talent, harnessing the best that the country could offer. The brightest of the best would be absorbed into the General Staff via the Military School for Officers (founded in 1810), soon to be known as the German Military School. Here the campaigns of 1806–7 were already being studied in great detail for their (largely negative) lessons. By 1859 this school would have evolved into the famous *Kriegsakademie*. The General Staff system had an early and decisively successful test when, on the evening of 16 June 1815, Grolman was able to encourage Gneisenau to take command of the Prussian Army on the field of Ligny after the incapacitation of Marshal von Blücher and lead it towards a union with the Anglo-Dutch-German Army two days later.

King Frederick William III, though a profound reactionary and deeply shocked by the independent action of Prussian generals during the Tauroggen Convention incident in 1812, was prepared to let the reformers continue their work in the army. In 1816 the General Staff was under the enlightened leadership of Grolman, who organised it into three geographic divisions – Eastern, Southern and Western. The officers in each studied the foreign armies, terrain, mobilisation and deployment in their spheres of operation, respectively covering the Russian, Austro-Hungarian and French armies. In 1817 a Fourth Division was added, especially for the study of military history. The General Staff evolved a Second Department comprising the Troop General Staff. These were officers rotating out of Berlin to serve as staff officers in corps and divisions across the nation (one per division; two or three per corps). The Berlin centre unofficially became known as the Great General Staff.

Grolman's four years in office, greatly assisted by War Minister Boyen, set the pattern for all future development of the staff system. He set a high intellectual standard, and instituted a scientific educa-tion, which encouraged individual study. As trained staff officers spread their influence throughout the army, they became talent spotters bringing suitable candidates to the attention of the chief of staff. Grolman paid great attention to the development of a good road system throughout the Prussian domains, and quickly saw the military usefulness of the spreading telegraph towers for the transmission of semaphore messages.

In 1819 the forces of reaction struck back as the Prussian and Austrian monarchs co-signed the Carlsbad Decrees designed to roll back the wave of liberal and nationalist reform in their territories. In a clash over whether the Landwehr should be a popular national militia or a Junker-led reserve force for the Royal Prussian Army, both Boyen and Grolman resigned their posts. There was a steep decline in the numbers of commoner officers as the Junker class re-established its control on the military. The General Staff managed to avoid too many adverse results; Clausewitz, always a more conservative officer than his colleagues, was made director of the Great War School, where he struggled to maintain high academic standards in the face of interference from old reactionaries.

In 1821 General Karl von Müffling became chief of staff of what was now officially known as the Great General Staff; by 1825 he had abolished the Second Department and was chief of both the Great and Troop General Staffs. He was a good and steady influence for gradual progressive change in a reactionary age but he could not prevent the department for personnel affairs re-emerging as a military cabinet to the king.

In the long peace from 1815 to 1864 the General Staff evolved as a collective brain able to operate outside the political reaction that had set in. Even the ultra-conservative War Minister Hake had enough practical military experience to recognise the increasing value of the General Staff. The king remained the commander-in-chief of the armed forces but it was the General Staff that provided all the intelligence and organisation on which any military operations were conducted.

Müffling did away with the geographic divisions and instituted a topic-based departmental system. The First Division dealt with personnel planning, in liaison with the War Ministry; the Second Division dealt with army organisation, manoeuvres, and deployment and mobilisation plans, also liaising with the training office of the War Ministry; the Third Division dealt with technology and artillery matters; the small Fourth Division dealt with military history. Only about twenty officers served on the Great General Staff, with another thirty-eight attached via their work in the Topographical and Trigonometric Bureaus. Some fifty General Staff-trained officers served in the wider army.

The Prussian Army remained acutely aware of the vulnerability of its nation's borders, both to the east and the west, and the need to plan for any eventuality. The Great General Staff planned in advance to bring the army to an operational readiness to meet the future hypothetical demands that might be made on it. It studied foreign armies (of both possible allies and enemies), military geography, the mobilisation of Prussia's troops and reserves, the expansion of sources of supply, men and *matériel* for the duration of war, the co-ordination and supervision of military plans and organisation in the various theatres of war, and the maintenance of operational readiness through training and doctrine (a function they increasingly influenced away from the War Ministry's Administration Department), together with the development of new technology and weaponry.

By influencing officer education in general, the General Staff was able to increase its influence and prestige. Officers selected by examination were taken in each year for further training; about one-third went on to serve on the staff at Berlin for two or three years. Only two or three of the very best remained as permanent Great General Staff officers – the rest returned to the army, where they were frequently singled out for 'fast track' promotion in both field and staff appointments.

Based on his study of the Great General Staff in the nineteenth century, Trevor Dupuy has devised this definition of a General Staff that still applies today:

> A General Staff is a highly trained, carefully selected group of military generalists whose function in peace or war is to assist the nation's military leadership – or a general commanding a field force of combined arms elements – in planning, controlling, directing, coordinating, and supervising the activities of all military subordinate elements in the most effective way possible, mutually supporting efforts to achieve an assigned goal or objective, or in maximum readiness to undertake such efforts. The leader or leadership makes decisions and gives commands; the General Staff's responsibility is to provide all possible support to assure that the decisions and commands are timely, sound, and effective.[1]

From 1829 to 1848 the chief of staff was the quietly competent General von Krauseneck, interestingly another ennobled commoner. He was quick to see the military importance of the electric telegraph. Similarly, when the first railway track was laid in Germany in 1835, it was less than two years later that the staff was studying its potential for accelerating troop mobilisation. The benefit of this enhancement to the internal lines of communications could have the greatest importance to Prussia's perennial problem of potential enemies on two open frontiers. Krauseneck gave the go-ahead for the introduction of the breech-loading rifle; for a shorter service in the ranks in order to increase the proportion of available young men to be trained, and the institutionalisation of war games (the *Kriegspiel* of the early 1820s) as a training tool for staff officers.

The revolutions that swept Europe in 1848 hardly affected the Prussian Army at all. The only long-term anomaly that would prove troublesome later was the granting of a small degree of democracy in Prussia, which left the minister of war (always a Prussian general) answerable both to his monarch and to the admittedly weak parliament. As German nationalists also advanced the idea of a united Germany with the Prussian king as their sovereign, Austria became increasingly alarmed and tension began to develop between the two German powers. Prussia was publicly humiliated by Austria's active intervention in south German affairs but chose not to act.

From 1848 to 1857 the chief of the General Staff was General Karl von Reyher, a long-serving and competent staff officer, an erudite student of military history who did much to increase the basic efficiency of the army. He knew that Prussian organisation and discipline would more than compensate for numerical inferiority and was ready to go to war at a moment's notice. In 1857 Reyher died suddenly and his monarch, Frederick William IV, had a severe stroke from which he never recovered. His soldier brother, Prince William, became regent and then king (and eventually emperor of Germany). One of his first acts was to appoint as chief of the General Staff General Helmuth von Moltke.

This gifted intellectual and writer spent sixty years of his life as an officer of the Great General Staff, after a total of only three years of regimental duty. He reorganised the staff into four main departments – Eastern (responsible for Russia, the non-German parts of the Austro-Hungarian Empire, Sweden and Turkey), German (Germany, Austria, Denmark, Switzerland and Italy), Western (France, Great Britain, Netherlands, Belgium, Spain and the USA) and, significantly, the Railway Department, which was tasked with co-ordinating the commercial development of railways with military needs. A Military History Department continued to exist separately to service all the other departments with historical studies to inform their work.

In 1859 the Prussian Army mobilised into the Rhineland by rail, with an eye to profiting from the Franco-Austrian war in northern Italy. That conflict ended rather suddenly and all Prussia could do was to study the campaign for posterity. Moltke led the work of his Military History Department in highlighting the tendency of commanders in the field to fight well enough in battle but to await further instructions when the situation was not so clear. He began formulating his idea that commanders should be given 'mission statements' and that formations should live and move separately and unite to fight.

From 1862 Prussia's new chancellor, Count Otto von Bismarck, began a conscious effort to unite Germany under Prussian leadership and against that of Austria. Still it was as German allies that Prussia and Austria went to war against Denmark in 1864, in defence of the right of the duchies of Schleswig and Holstein to reject a new Danish king. The thinly-veiled contempt of the old Prussian generals for the bookish Great General Staff was shown by Field Marshal Friedrich von Wrangel taking the reactionary Vogel von Falckenstein, who had never been selected by the General Staff, to be his chief of staff. He studiously ignored Moltke, who was kept informed of operations by a General Staff colonel serving in Prince Frederick Charles's corps. After some warnings against violating Danish territory proper had been ignored, Falckenstein was replaced as chief of staff by Moltke. Eventually Prince Frederick Charles replaced Wrangel and, with

Moltke to plan things smoothly, the war was swiftly brought to a close.

Moltke, now aged 64, would have been content to retire but King William would have none of that. Bismarck then moved in a cold and efficient way to first isolate Austria diplomatically, and then to manufacture a *casus belli*. Austria and her south German allies had a great numerical advantage but Moltke knew that he could mobilise his technically superior field army twice as fast as his opponents could muster theirs. Prussia even allowed other belligerents to mobilise ahead of them, to enhance the fiction that it did not desire war. With a deadly efficiency Prussia demanded the neutrality of Saxony, Hanover and Hesse-Kassel, received the expected rejections and promptly overwhelmed them. Meanwhile Moltke led (in the name of the king) three widely spread Prussian armies in a converging invasion of Bohemia. He 'commanded' the three armies from the end of the telegraph lines in Berlin. Not until 30 June 1866 did he go forward, with the Royal headquarters, to oversee the final encirclement and destruction of Benedek's Austrian Army. We should, at this stage, demolish the old canard that a Prussian divisional commander queried an order received in Moltke's name because he had no idea who he was. Not only would the name of the chief of the Great General Staff be known to every Prussian formation commander, but that same chief of staff would have absolutely no business sending an order to a divisional commander who had both an army and a corps commander through whom that sort of thing would be routed.

Prince Frederick Charles's First Army pinned the Austrian Army in the centre around Sadowa and Moltke moved decisively to hurry the Second Army onto the battlefield. The Army of the Elbe marched too directly onto the field and spoiled the chance of a complete encirclement. Austrian cavalry covered the retreat of a thoroughly beaten army. Bismarck pushed through a quick and fairly generous peace. Moltke's faith in the Prussian system of independently minded commanders, assisted by uniformly trained staff officers, had stood up to its first real test. Of course some things went wrong. Moltke famously said that no plan survives first contact with the enemy. But the system worked and victory was rarely in doubt.

Immediately the Military History Department got to work on the campaign, drawing important lessons for the improvement of the organisation and training of the army. The Prussian cavalry needed to grasp the importance of reconnaissance and surveillance, of screening the movements of the army and the denying of intelligence to the enemy cavalry by active patrolling. The Prussian cavalry had been execrable in that respect. The error of holding the artillery at the rear of long infantry columns was also corrected. The admirably aggressive Prussian infantry often found itself badly disorganised at the end of a fight and a good deal of thought was given to keeping better control during the battle, and to the proper flow of information between fighting units and their higher commanders, and between units in the firing line. The huge increase in the lethality of the rifle over earlier muskets had to be worked into new tactics. As early as mid 1865 Moltke had already deduced, based on his deep understanding of the often referred to but little read *On War* by Clausewitz, that the increasing power of the defence given to it by modern firepower imposed a new ideal on campaigning in the field. The strategic offensive to seize the initiative and select an advantageous battlefield should lead to a tactical defensive in which the enemy would be obliged to attack, suffer a repulse and become vulnerable to a counterstroke by reserves kept in hand for that purpose.

As chief of the General Staff, Moltke could only make recommendations to the army. His close relationship with War Minister General Albrecht von Roon, meant that the relevant inspector generals were soon applying the new techniques in the light of recent war experience.

The Great General Staff was reorganised in 1867 into a Main Establishment and a Supporting Establishment. The former retained the three geographical departments – First Department (Austria,

Russia, Scandinavia, Turkey, Greece and Asia), Second Department (Prussia, Germany, Switzerland and Italy) and Third Department (France, Great Britain, Belgium, Holland, Spain, Portugal and America). The Second Department included the Railway Section whose work became so vital that it was expanded into a full department in its own right. The supporting departments were five in number: Military History, Geographical-Statistical, Topographical, War Room, and Land Triangulation Bureau.

The armies of north Germany were integrated into the Prussian military system and Bismarck's diplomacy began to prepare for a war with France, which was engineered through an anachronistic dispute over a pro-German candidate for the Spanish throne. Prussia deployed 380,000 troops in three armies that concentrated towards the French frontier between 20 and 30 July 1870. Uncertainty over the attitude of Austria and Italy meant that 95,000 first-line troops had to be retained in the interior. The wide and separate deployment of the field armies was intended to lure the French Army – eight independent army corps under the general command of the Emperor Napoleon III and General Leboeuf (the war minister) – into an encirclement trap. The overly aggressive General Karl von Steinmetz (First Army) sprung the trap too soon by attacking the leading French troops at Saarbrücken. The French halted their forward movement and belatedly reorganised into two armies – five corps in and around Metz under Marshal Bazaine, and three in Alsace under Marshal MacMahon.

Prussian armies were directed by clear-headed and well-practiced staffs; French armies by hastily organised and ill-trained ad hoc staffs. The outcome was a foregone conclusion, allowing for the normal frictions of war and the stubborn courage of men in battle.

In the field Moltke operated with a contingent drawn from the Great General Staff in Berlin – fourteen General Staff officers, ten cartographers, seven clerks, and fifty-nine other rank messengers and assistant clerks. These served alongside the much larger Royal household, with its large number of advisers from the Ministry of War. Two of these, the quartermaster general and the intendant general, worked closely and well with the Field General Staff. The first use of the term 'demigods' to describe officers of the Great General Staff applied to Moltke's three section chiefs – Colonel Paul von Schellendorf of the operations and movement section, Colonel Karl von Brandenstein of the railway and supply section, and Colonel Julius von Verdy du Vernois of the intelligence section.

Despite repeated displays of battlefield courage, and the occasional blunder by the victors, the French armies were overwhelmed by Prussian armies working in concert to a planned system of operations (which is not the same as working to a single predetermined plan). The care and attention paid by the Prussian officer corps at all levels to the training of their troops for war, their diligent retention of the initiative in the field, the transformation of the Prussian cavalry into an excellent instrument for patrolling and screening, and the aggressive forward deployment of massed and co-ordinated artillery all combined to bring the French field armies to total defeat in just four weeks.

French studies of their defeat acknowledge that this formidable military machine was directed by the best intellects available to the Prussian Army through the school of excellence that was the Great General Staff. Moltke displayed no great flashes of genius that one might expect from a 'great captain' of history. Instead he organised and set in motion a force that operated with a calm and deadly efficiency with which he preferred not to interfere. The use of the tactical defensive in battle during the overall strategic offensive was a huge success.

To Prussia's great surprise the French people under the spirited leadership of Gambetta refused to accept defeat and resisted for several months more, putting armies of new levies into the field and into inevitable defeat against the German veterans. During this phase there were repeated clashes between the Prussian military leaders, who insisted on being left to finish the campaign in their own way, and the government of Chancellor Bismarck, which obviously viewed military operations only in the light of the wider political perspective. For all his pioneering practice of Clausewitz's theories on war, Moltke had an imperfect understanding of the primacy of the political direction of the war, and that the purely military point of view should be subordinated to political imperatives throughout. Without this, war for its own sake simply has no point. Already that fatal flaw in the Prussian military/political system, whereby the military demanded unfettered control of policy until the fighting was settled, had emerged. It would be both the foundation and the destruction of the German Empire. Military authorities everywhere often look upon the policy demands of civilian governments as meddling in affairs best left to the experts. In the shallow and imperfect democracy of late nineteenth- and early twentieth-century Germany this failure of political control of such a mighty arm of the State would lead to a disastrous inability to organise the nation in its greatest test.

After three victorious wars the prestige and popularity of the army in the new German Empire could not have been higher. It was still the emperor's army, operating independently of the civilian governmental process, but it was universally held to be the best in the world (and was copied in many places, if only in the widespread adoption of the *pickelhaube* helmet. Professional General Staffs would be a more substantial imitation in the years to come).

The army of a united Germany was modelled on the Prussian system and for the next forty-three years, guided by the enormous prestige of the Great General Staff, it would prepare itself for a war of any eventuality. The General Staff took full and direct responsibility for officer education, and for Germany's Directorate of Communications and Railways. The chief of the General Staff was now, though still unofficially, the principal military adviser to the Kaiser, thanks largely to the excellent relationship he shared with the minister of war and the chief of the Military Cabinet. The Great General Staff carefully watched the work of the War Ministry and made numerous recommendations to guide its work of creating a unified and uniformly trained army. The Military History Department fed its studies directly into the curriculum of the *Kriegsakademie*, the officer and non-commissioned officer schools, and into the work of the inspector generals responsible for training programmes.

It was the work of the historians, and the study of the results of the autumn manoeuvres and the annual staff rides, that finally crystallised into the official adoption of 'mission based' orders and tactics (*auftragstaktik*). Moltke's own words on the subject were incorporated into the training manuals: 'A favourable situation will never be exploited if commanders wait for orders. The highest commander and the youngest soldier must always be conscious of the fact that omission and inactivity are worse than resorting to the wrong expedient'.[2] Moltke enjoyed illustrating this point by recounting an incident he observed on a visit to the headquarters of Prince Frederick Charles. Defending himself against charges of a battlefield blunder, a Prussian major retorted that he had been obeying the orders of a senior officer as if they had come from the king himself. The prince famously chided him by replying, 'His Majesty made you a major because he believed you would know when *not* to obey his orders'.

Each department of the Great General Staff kept to its work perfecting aspects of the German military system. The operations section of each department routinely studied all contemporary military 'problems' and drew up contingency plans for mobilisation and employment to meet any and all eventualities. This would certainly cover every nation bordering Germany, and the idea of trampling down the neutrality of Belgium, Luxembourg, the Netherlands and/or Denmark would have been of no consequence whatsoever to an 'apolitical' General Staff planning officer interested only in the correct military solution to said military problem. Even an attack on the United States of America was planned in this perfectly routine way, just in case it should ever prove necessary. In his later reflections on the Gallipoli campaign, Sir Ian Hamilton wrote that, if he had been a German general, he would have been handed a complete order of battle and detailed analysis of his own forces, an up-to-date study of the enemy forces and the terrain and resources of the theatre of war, and an outline plan of campaign and all the necessary preparations. Hamilton contrasts this with the derisory lack of information he received from a War Office staff as ill-prepared as he was for the Gallipoli adventure.

Germany's principal military problem after 1871 was, of course, the French desire for revenge and the recovery of the lost provinces of Alsace and Lorraine. The danger of France making common cause with Tsarist Russia to put pressure on Germany would open up the nightmare possibility of a war with great powers simultaneously on two fronts. The near extinction of Frederick the Great in the Seven Years' War was the example to be avoided at all costs. Austria remained a potential enemy after her 1866 defeat. Moltke originally planned to oppose France and Russia equally using the strategic offensive/tactical defensive so recently perfected to place German armies on the territory of their enemies and defeat their frenzied counter-attacks there. Chancellor Bismarck's diplomacy did much to relieve Germany of such worries. His *Dreikaiserbund,* trying to unite the interests of Germany, Austria and Russia, did not survive Austro-Russian rivalries in the Balkans. Germany and Austria became allies as a result of the Russo-Turkish war of 1877–8. The League of the Three Emperors was revived in 1881 and, to complete France's isolation, Italy was drawn into an alliance with Germany and Austria.

It wasn't long before Moltke recognised that France's faster and more determined mobilisation plans posed the greater threat. He began planning for a massive deployment against France, a quick decision in the West, and then the rapid transfer of large forces to the East to deal with the ponderous Russian Army. The Great General Staff began a series of demands for the expansion of the German standing army, which still needed a Reichstag vote to approve the necessary funding, to meet these new strategic commitments. This hugely important strategic decision would dominate German military thinking until 1914. Staff talks with the Austrians would sometimes see it tilt towards dealing with the Russians first; the promise of six Italian corps on the Rhine would see the emphasis swing back to dealing with France first.

Moltke, when he was 82 years old, groomed the quartermaster general, General Count Alfred von Waldersee, as his successor. Waldersee was of that Great General Staff persuasion that resented its constitutional subordination to the war minister, and an alliance soon formed with the Military Cabinet to undermine the influence of the Prussian War Ministry. Even Chancellor Bismarck, fearing the rise of liberal and socialist numbers in the Reichstag, harboured doubts about the future reliability of the war minister. Their combined attack forced the resignation of a war minister (von Kameke) in 1883 and the transfer of all matters pertaining to military personnel from the Ministry to the emperor's Military Cabinet. This was part of that fatal process that detached German military policy from any pretence of political control, let alone democratic control, and would ultimately be disastrous for both the army and the nation.

The year 1888 saw the accession of Kaiser Wilhelm II, the eventual retirement of Moltke and the confirmation of Waldersee as chief of staff. This born intriguer was soon at odds with the Military Cabinet, the War Ministry and the chancellor. He cleverly had a friend, Major General Wilhelm von Hahnke, appointed as chief of the Military Cabinet. Then War Minister Bronsart von Schellendorf found himself increasingly bypassed as Wilhelm II took all his military advice from the Military Cabinet and the Great General Staff. Schellendorf resigned over this lack of access to the emperor; his successor, Verdy du Vernois, soon followed this course of action. This battle for access to the 'supreme warlord' would soon see the back of Waldersee himself because of his opposition to increased spending on the navy, and to the dismissal of Bismarck as chancellor in 1890.

The new chief of the Great General Staff was General Count Alfred von Schlieffen (1833–1913), a law student who took to the military life after service as a one-year volunteer. His keen intellect saw him fill numerous regimental and staff appointments with distinction and, in the 1880s, he was being consciously groomed as successor to Moltke and Waldersee. He eschewed all politics and intrigue and concentrated on preparing the army for any war it might be called upon to fight. He was a profound student of military history and he became the leading advocate of the encircling manoeuvre designed to bring about a battle of annihilation (the so-called 'Cannae solution', after Hannibal's crushing victory over the Romans in 216 BC). By manoeuvre, and by ceaselessly seeking to outflank the enemy, quick and decisive victory could be assured. He held that the lessons of 1812 denied the chance of first-strike success against Russia and so favoured the Western strategy, with anything up to 90 per cent of the German Army committed to fighting France in the first stages of any new conflict.

Schlieffen embraced new technology as 'force multipliers', with increased importance attached to railways and heavy artillery. He created the German Army's corps of railway engineers to push the railheads forwards behind his advancing troops; the heavier guns were required to deal with evermore sophisticated concrete fortifications.

As Germany watched republican France and Tsarist Russia become allies, and draw Great Britain into their triple Entente, the German war plan solidified into what is now known as the Schlieffen Plan. Light forces would cover East Prussia against the slowly mobilising Russians. In the West, Alsace-Lorraine would be protected by relatively light forces while the mass of the German Army wheeled around the open French flank, violating Belgian, Luxembourg and Dutch neutrality if necessary, and discounting the possible intervention of Great Britain which might result from this action. Thus the 'non-political', purely military requirements of the plan would have the greatest possible political (and hence grand strategical) consequences. This lack of political control over the workings of the Great General Staff was a fatal flaw that affected its performance repeatedly in its history. The seizing of the initiative and the imposing of one's own campaign strategy on the enemy was of the highest importance. Schlieffen fully understood that the offensive into the home territory of a modern enemy would soon lose impetus, unless massive trained reserves were on hand to keep up the tempo of operations. The Great General Staff stepped up the pressure for increases in the army estimates and in the size of the standing army.

When Schlieffen retired, Wilhelm II insisted on having his very own Moltke to replace him and so the nephew of the great man, General Helmuth von Moltke 'the Younger', took up the reins. He genuinely did not want the job, admitting to anyone who would listen that he wasn't up to it. He amended 'the Plan', refusing to violate Dutch neutrality (and staking everything on the early seizure of Liège to allow the passage of the armies into northern France). He also reinforced the defence of Alsace, Lorraine and the German frontiers in the south, that only contributed to a weakening of the *masse de manoeuvre* in the north. The 'Napoleonic boldness' of Schlieffen's bid for a swift and decisive knockout blow was steadily eroded. But these were purely military considerations of a hypothetical conflict that might or might not occur. The German military system stood poised to carry out whatever task was asked of it by a political leadership so thoroughly outdated and outmoded in the new twentieth century. As parliamentarism and nationalism, democracy and socialism became evermore potent forces on the world stage, the German Army continued to serve a feudal warlord and his retainers as his personal weapon.

It was a weapon directed by a college of experts, all rooted in the regimental system of the army, but highly trained and like-minded in their approach to the solving of military problems. The key to their expertise and their success was the constant striving to analyse every new experience and adapt lessons for the further organisation and training of the army. Between 1914 and 1918 they would demonstrate their excellence in this analytical approach to warfare, but would also see their efforts dissipated as the army seized unto itself the entire running of the nation state.

This system produced in Hindenburg a solid and reliable practitioner of the military art, deeply imbued with the principles of war and a fine leader of men. In Ludendorff it found a man with a genius for war and a seemingly insatiable need to work, pushing himself and those around him to the limits of their endurance. The calm and placid nature of the one was often needed to stabilise the excitable and nervous aspect of the other. It is small wonder that they were seen as an inseparable duo.

*chapter two*

# Two Roads to Tannenberg

The Prussian royalist who was to become the president of a German republic and whose name was to become a household word and be used to christen airships, whole villages and every manner of commercial product, was listed in the Prussian Army lists under 'B'. The Beneck-endorffs were an ancient Brandenburg military family dating from the thirteenth century, and as Teutonic Knights they went crashing down to defeat at the hands of a Polish-Lithuanian and Slavic army at the battle of Tannenberg in 1410. In their centuries of military service no less than twenty-three Beneckendorffs died on the field of battle. It was a Beneckendorff cousin serving on the German Great General Staff in 1914 who was to recommend the retired general for the posting that was to make him one of the two most famous Germans of the twentieth century.

The Hindenburgs also traced their military ancestry back to the Teutonic Knights and the battle of Tannenberg. For their services in the Silesian wars (1740–56) the Hindenburgs were rewarded by their king, Frederick the Great, with two estates in the West Prussian Neumark. In particular a Colonel Hindenburg had lost his leg in battle to a cannon ball that might easily have struck the great king. The estates of Limbsee and Neudeck were an important addition to the finances of this typically cash-poor Junker family. The former had to be sold as the family reorganised its finances after the Napoleonic Wars, but Neudeck remained with them until the Weimar era.

In 1789 a Royal decree allowed the request of the old, unmarried Colonel Hindenburg to leave his estates to his great-nephew Beneck-endorff, provided the two names were joined and thus it was Paul Ludwig Hans Anton von Beneckendorff und von Hindenburg who was born at Posen on 2 October 1847 and it was by the former name that he was usually known.

It was a misfortune for the family that a Major Ernst Ludwig Beneckendorff, a cousin of Hindenburg's grandfather, had failed his great test in war and had surrendered fortress Spandau to the French during the calamitous days after the twin defeats of Jena and Auerstadt in 1806. After great bluster about defending the place until it was in ruins (in all truth it already was), he allowed a council of war to agree to surrender on a number of paltry pretexts. He was court-martialled in 1808 and was condemned to be shot for this grave dereliction of duty. The king of Prussia commuted the sentence to life imprisonment in a fortress. The Prussian monarchy had a long and unforgiving memory for such blots on a family record.

The von Beneckendorff und von Hindenburg family was a classic product of the Prussian Junker system. They were of a landowning class, never particularly wealthy on the produce of the difficult Prussian soil, but maintained in a privileged position in society by their utter personal dedication to the service of the kings of Prussia. Their almost universal service in the army was a 'social contract' they had with the monarchy and they served with a religious zeal that was largely unques-tioning because it was a truly symbiotic relationship. There was more than a hint of truth in the 'Junker' jingle: 'Absolute shall reign the king, obeying us in everything'. Compared to many ruling elites they lived a Spartan existence, and childhood and schooling was directed towards the service of the Prussian state. Though their estate workers no longer endured serfdom (only abolished in 1807), they still held enormous power over their lives and accepted the deference of the common people with an easy grace. Command came naturally to them.

With his father completely absorbed in his military duties, moving from one garrison post to another and never seeing active service, Paul von Beneckendorff und von Hindenburg was raised by a formidable nurse, who knew her duty well and ended all misbehaviour by roaring, 'Silence in the ranks!' He absorbed the tales of military glory from his loving grandparents at Neudeck, along with a distaste for the middle classes who were becoming increasingly wealthy and insistent on a political role in the state. Ironically there was a hint of bourgeois blood in the veins of the great Hindenburg, through which he inherited his imposing physique. Through his maternal grandmother he was descended from one of the 'giant' Potsdam Grenadiers of Frederick William I, and his grandfather on that side had served well against the French in 1813. These 'common' ancestors were entirely worthy Prussians but are never referred to in the slightest way in any of the Hindenburg family writings.

It is hard to imagine, given the taciturn nature of the elder statesman, that young Paul was noted as a chatterbox at school. In 1858, aged 11, he joined the Prussian Cadet Corps, which institution existed from 1717 to 1919 to begin the training of the sons of the Junkers for army service. The serious little chap wrote his last will and testament before he left home, carefully assigning his toys to various siblings and asking that an impoverished friend continue to receive the bread roll that Paul had been giving him daily, and concluding with the words: 'I hereby confirm that I have written the above in all truth and sincerity'. As a sort of codicil he added: 'Peace and quiet is what I pray may henceforward be granted me'.[1] An early sign, perhaps, of that calmness and placidity that was to be the chief characteristic of his personality. He remembered the discipline as 'consciously and purposely rough' and he absorbed the caste-like honour code that embraced the whole German officer corps. It was a narrow and intensive schooling. All the lessons – geography, history, French, mathematics – were based solely on military examples. The humanities were regarded as time-wasting anathema. After attending the cadet school at Wahlstatt for five years, he transferred to the central school at Berlin in 1863. His military education continued there until 1866, when he briefly served as a page of honour to the widowed Queen Elizabeth of Prussia. She gave him a gold watch that he would wear all the days of his life. Aged 19, he was commissioned into the Third Regiment of Foot Guards as a second lieutenant.

Like all officers in the Prussian Army, he swore a deeply symbolic personal oath to serve his king:

> I, Paul Ludwig Hans Anton von Beneckendorff und von Hindenburg, hereby personally swear to God the Omniscient and Almighty that I shall faithfully and loyally serve His Majesty the King of Prussia, my most gracious sovereign, on any and every occasion, on land or at sea, in war and peace, and at every place whatsoever: that I shall further the All-Highest's best advantage, while averting from him injury and disadvantage; that I shall closely abide by the articles of war, which have been read to me, and precisely obey the orders I receive; and that I shall so conduct myself as it behoves an upright, fearless, dutiful, and honourable soldier. So help me God through Jesus Christ and His Holy Gospel.[2]

He was soon on active service in the war against Austria. His regiment, only formed in 1860, moved to Potsdam to join the Guards Corps assembling there. He took care to take his platoon to see the tomb of Frederick the Great. His first taste of action came on 28 June in the combat at the Soor, where his battalion skirmished through some woods against Austrian infantry and then repulsed a charge by two squadrons of Austrian *uhlans*, capturing their transport and the regimental chest and papers. On 3 July 1866 his unit marched to the sound of the guns and participated in the battle of Königgrätz. As the regiment debouched from the valley of the Elbe it came under artillery fire. His company commander was wounded and his senior NCO was killed. After a sharp firefight put some Austrian infantry to flight, he led his platoon in hot pursuit, soon leaving his battalion far behind. They burst upon an Austrian battery deployed in a field and attacked them immediately. In that fight he was wounded, a bullet passing through the eagle plate of his *pickelhaube* and grazing his head. His loving parents had secreted a biblical text behind the helmet plate and their religious faith was rewarded. He was unconscious for a while but came to in time to see his men secure the capture of five out of the eight guns. Forced to take cover by Austrian rifle fire, they were well placed to ambush some retreating Austrian cavalry. After rejoining their unit they were heavily engaged in the defence of Rosberitz, being driven out of the village before rallying and completing its capture. The battle was won and, within three weeks, his regiment was approaching Vienna when the war ended successfully. He was subsequently decorated with the Order of the Red Eagle in time for the triumphal march into Berlin. He had been considered for the prestigious *Pour le Mérite* but was thought to be too young for it.

The next four years were spent at Hanover with the regiment, a ceaseless round of training the annual intake of recruits. His combat experience made him one of the celebrities of the regiment and he was noted for the highly realistic nature of his training. He rose to be a lieutenant in the Franco-Prussian War (1870–1) and his consistently brave performance, especially at the battle of Gravelotte-St Privat, earned him the Iron Cross. Here, as adjutant to the battalion, he spent the whole battle on horseback beside his commanding officer and was lucky to remain unscathed. In the famous charge of the Prussian Guards at St Privat his regiment lost sixty-four officers and 1,064 men in the space of one hour. Seventy per cent of the unit's officers were killed. When his battalion commander succeeded to command of the regiment, he became adjutant to the regiment. He observed the battle at Sedan, from where he wrote to his parents about how careful the German soldiers had to be not to violate the sovereign territory of Belgium! After service at the siege of Paris he was honoured by being chosen by his regiment to represent them at the proclamation of the German emperor in the Hall of Mirrors at Versailles.

Of all the European great powers, Germany saw the least overseas military activity in the next forty-three years. Hindenburg would spend forty of those years in the army, gradually working his way to senior rank through a succession of regimental, staff and higher commands. His most enthusiastic biographers describe his performance as 'valuable, though not decisive'. He conscientiously contributed to the perfecting of the German military machine. He held duty to be above ambition. He read only military books and took little interest in any other topics, except hunting.

After two years regimental duty and study at Hanover he was admitted as a student to the War Academy in 1873. After early complaints at being made to study ancient history instead of modern tactics, he settled down to his work. That he absorbed the ethos of the German system is revealed in his writing: 'The first requirement in a General Staff Officer was to subordinate his individuality and his actions to the general welfare'.[3] Joining the circle of friends around Prince Alexander of Prussia, he fondly remembered meeting the great Field Marshal Moltke at the prince's house. Graduating from the War Academy in 1877, he returned to regimental duty at Hanover, before becoming a captain on the General Staff. He was transferred to Stettin and, as the youngest staff officer on the post, was given a great deal of very detailed work to do. He relished the challenge and became well versed in the intricacies of the movement and well-being of the troops, and did well as aide-de-camp to senior officers on instructional staff rides. At Stettin, aged 32, he married the daughter of the distinguished General von Sperling. In the only mention of his wife in his memoirs, the field marshal described her, after a long, faithful and harmonious marriage, as 'my best friend and comrade'. His only son would become a soldier; his two daughters would marry soldiers.

From 1881 to 1885 he was a staff officer at Königsberg (under General Verdy du Vernois) and later at Posen. Here he acquired his detailed knowledge of the defence problems of the eastern frontiers of the German Empire. General Verdy du Vernois was no idle flatterer; his remark in a letter to the chief of staff, Waldersee, in 1884 that 'Beneckendorff' was a man on whom the General Staff could set great hopes is significant. He was promoted to major on the General Staff in 1885 and worked at Berlin under General Schlieffen, and he was an instructor in tactics at the War Academy for a while. Later, even some of his critics would recall what a profound knowledge and understanding he had of military history. Since Verdy du Vernois was a renowned military historian, known for his study of not how campaigns went but how they ought to have gone (the 'counter-factual approach') we can see that Hindenburg had the best possible support in his work. He contributed greatly to the new Field Service Regulations, writing most of the section on the work of mixed bodies of troops himself. When Verdy du Vernois became minister of war in 1889, he followed his old chief to the ministry in Berlin where he headed the department of General War Administration, with particular responsibility for the development of military engineering and heavy artillery. He was well versed in the latest technical innovations but wisely observed: 'Don't forget that it is the man himself who is the decisive factor, and that the only use of the machine is to intensify the effect of his action. The will is what matters. It is the character of the fighter which enables him to use his weapons to the best advantage'.[4]

After four more years of intensely detailed staff work, where he remembered his unique contribution was a memorandum on the use of heavy artillery in field warfare, he was pleased to return to his old regiment as its commander in 1893. He was now one of some two to three hundred officers destined for the highest levels of command. In

1896, promoted to major general, he was chief of staff to the Grand
Duke of Baden's Eighth Army Corps at Coblenz, and worked on contingency plans for the defence of the East whilst there; in 1900, on the
recommendation of the Grand Duke, he was the commander of the
28th Division at Karlsruhe. By 1902 he was IV Corps commander at
Magdeburg and would serve there until his retirement from the army in
1911. He was now responsible for the careers of a thousand officers
under his command and he was remembered as a strict but fair commander. He met his staff officers twice a week and left them to get on
with their work; he was famously a good listener and favoured clarity
and terseness of expression at all times. If his attention to the punctu-
ation in documents seemed a little pedantic, he reminded his staff
officers that an action had once been lost because a misplaced comma
left an order unclear. He preached care and attention towards the rank
and file; he was known to cancel a church parade if his soldiers were
dog-tired from their exercises. His speeches were slow and deliberate; he
eschewed oratory in favour of clarity in communicating his intentions.
There was nothing hasty or excitable about him; he was a calming influence on all within his sphere of action. His memory was very good, and
he firmly believed that nervous energy was an asset to be conserved for
times of crisis. Quite simply he liked his sleep and would not be deprived
of it under any circumstance. Throughout his service at Magdeburg
he was remembered by all who knew him as 'patient, good natured,
dispassionate, and thoroughly efficient both as teacher and organiser'.[5]
He was strict, especially in matters of dress, but also fair and just.

He might have been routinely considered for the post of chief of
the Great General Staff when the chief of the Military Cabinet sounded
him out about it in 1903 but he expressed an aversion to working so
closely with the court. In 1909 he was also considered for the post of
Prussia's war minister.

The exact reason for his retirement is not clear, though he was, of
course, 64-years old by then. Popular opinion has it that he made the

mistake of allowing the army corps commanded by the Kaiser in person to lose the 1908 manoeuvres; not a good career move! But his age is a more likely explanation. He personally insisted that:

> … the decision to leave the army matured within me gradually. I had attained far more in my military career than I had ever dared hope for. There was no war in sight, and so I recognised it as my duty to make room for younger officers. For this reason I asked to be retired in 1911. As a false legend has arisen around the unimportant fact of my retirement, I should like expressly to declare that no professional or personal friction caused me to take this step.[6]

On his retirement he was awarded the exalted Order of the Black Eagle by a Kaiser who might be his true and legitimate supreme warlord but for whom he had not a great personal regard. He already felt that Wilhelmine Germany was losing some of its old virtues. He wrote to his son, newly commissioned into his old regiment of Foot Guards, with advice that may reflect some of these concerns: 'We are not made officers, moreover, to ride the high horse as regards the rank and file'.

He spent his retirement between a home in Hanover and his estate in the East. He did not, as John Buchan would have us believe, spend it studying the forest paths in and around the Masurian Lakes in some supernatural prediction of his great moment in the future, though as a General Staff officer he would have known the area well enough. Instead he put on a little weight and read the newspapers as many are wont to do. He kept up his studies of military history and took a keen (pro-Turkish) interest in the Balkan Wars. When war did break out on 4 August 1914 he volunteered his services but was disappointed not to be recalled to the colours immediately; he held himself in readiness for any task he might be asked to do.

From the archetypal Prussian Junker officer, we now turn to that other mainstay of the German officer corps – the gifted commoner. Erich Ludendorff was born on 9 April 1865 at Kruschevnia in the Posen area (coincidentally close to where Hindenburg was born). His father was descended from Pomeranian merchants and had become a landowner in a modest sort of way and held a commission in the reserve cavalry. His mother was from the noble but impoverished von Templehoff family. Erich was the third of six children and had a stable and comfortable childhood. He was a lonely boy at school; an obsessive desire for cleanliness separated him from his peers and a flair for mathematics steered him towards bookishness. His father was delighted when he elected early on for a military career. In 1877, aged 12, he passed the entrance examinations for the Cadet School at Plon with distinction, based mainly on his excellent mathematics results. He was placed in a class two years ahead of his actual age. He preferred to forego the pleasures of the sports field and gymnasium and forged ahead academically. In 1880 he moved to the Military Academy at Lichterfelde, near Berlin. His devotion to study intensified, while many of his fellow students seemed more interested in gambling, drinking, and duelling. An iron self-discipline kept him working harder and harder as he absorbed the Prussian model of leadership and service in its entirety; he was consistently first in his class. In 1885 he was commissioned as a second lieutenant in the 57th Infantry Regiment at Wesel. Over the next eight years he saw further service as a lieutenant with the 2nd Marine Battalion at Kiel and Wilhelmshaven, and the 8th Grenadier Guards at Frankfurt on the Oder. His service reports were of the highest order, with frequent commendations. He was selected for the War Academy in 1893 where the commandant, General Meckel, recommended him for appointment to the General Staff. He was a captain in 1895, sent to command an infantry company at Thorn; then to staff appointments with 9th Division at Glogau and V Corps at Posen. He was a major by 1900 and was a senior staff officer with V Corps headquarters from 1902 to 1904.

His widely acknowledged brilliance led to the call to join the Great General Staff in Berlin under the leadership of Schlieffen, whom

Ludendorff admired as 'one of the greatest soldiers who ever lived'. In 1905 he joined the Second Section, responsible for the mobilisation and concentration of the German armies at the outbreak of war. In 1907 he was made a lieutenant colonel; in 1908 he was selected ahead of the able (but non-Prussian) Walter Groener to be head of the Second Section. He was intimately involved in the evolution and perfecting of arrangements for the famous Schlieffen Plan.

The new Kaiser, Wilhelm II, had dispensed with the services of Count Otto von Bismarck (famously depicted in a Punch cartoon as 'Dropping the Pilot') and Germany's overall strategic position had gone from bad to worse. Germany's close alliance with Austria-Hungary threw Tsarist Russia into the arms of the French and the Great General Staff was faced with its worst nightmare – a possible war on two fronts against two major powers. In 1905 Schlieffen presented his solution to this age-old problem, based on studies he had conducted since 1897. Assuming that Russia would be slow to mobilise, a small covering force would be left in the East (barely one-ninth of Germany's mobilised strength) which would expect to engage the Russians in and around the Masurian Lakes before falling back slowly to the line of the Vistula. The overwhelming mass of the German armed forces would attack France and endeavour to overthrow her armies in a matter of six weeks. On the Western Front, Alsace Lorraine, rather like East Prussia, would be lightly covered and may well have to face invasion while the German field armies swept down on Paris and outflanked the entire French Army.

Ludendorff embraced this doctrine enthusiastically. Like all good Germans he saw no alternative to preparation for war: 'In our unfavourable military-political position in the centre of Europe, sur-rounded by enemies, we had to reckon with foes greatly superior in numbers and prepare ourselves accordingly, if we did not wish to allow ourselves to be crushed'.[7] That the plans he was working on involved the violation of Belgian neutrality (and the possible drawing of Great Britain into a coalition against Germany) was, in the best traditions of

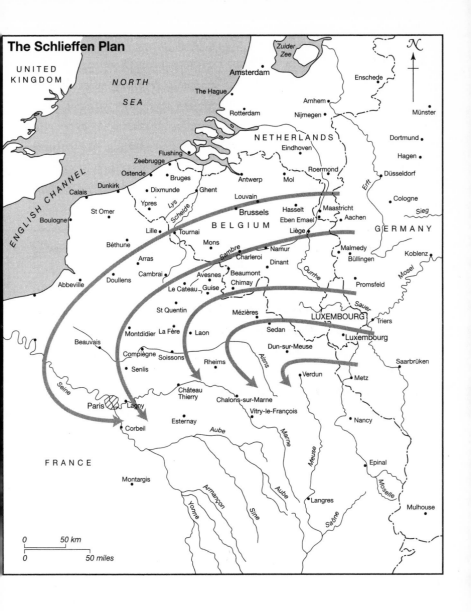

The Schlieffen Plan

UNITED
KINGDOM

NORTH
SEA

NETHERLANDS

Amsterdam

The Hague

Rotterdam

Zuider
Zee

Enschede

Arnhem

Nijmegen

Münster

Eindhoven

Roermond

Dortmund

Hagen

Düsseldorf

Cologne

Sieg

GERMANY

ENGLISH CHANNEL

Flushing

Zeebrugge

Ostende

Bruges

Dunkirk

Dixmunde

Calais

Ypres

Lys

Schelde

Boulogne

St Omer

Lille

Tournai

Ghent

Antwerp

Mol

Louvain

Brussels

Hasselt

Maastricht

Eben Emael

Liège

Aachen

BELGIUM

Mons

Namur

Sambre

Charleroi

Dinant

Malmedy

Büllingen

Koblenz

Béthune

Arras

Cambrai

Avesnes

Beaumont

Le Cateau

Guise

Chimay

Ourthe

Mosel

Abbeville

Doullens

Promsfeld

St Quentin

Mézières

Sauer

LUXEMBOURG

Triers

Beauvais

Montdidier

La Fère

Laon

Sedan

Luxembourg

Compiègne

Soissons

Rheims

Dun-sur-Meuse

Saarbrüken

Senlis

Aisne

Verdun

Metz

Seine

Paris

Lagny

Château
Thierry

Chalons-sur-Marne

Vitry-le-François

Nancy

Corbeil

Esternay

Aube

Marne

Meuse

Epinal

FRANCE

Montargis

Armançon

Yonne

Sine

Aube

Saône

Langres

Moselle

Mulhouse

0      50 km

0                    50 miles

the Great General Staff, of no consequence to him whatsoever. He rationalised the situation by assuming that France would not respect Belgian neutrality either, or that Belgium would join the anti-German coalition. This aspect of the plan would involve Ludendorff personally in ways he could not imagine as he slaved away over railway timetables, and the march tables and supply arrangements of dozens of converging army corps.

The new chief of the Great General Staff, Colonel General Helmuth von Moltke (nephew of the great Moltke, and inevitably known as Moltke the Younger) had very reluctantly accepted the post at the insistence of the Kaiser when Schlieffen retired in 1905. In a remarkably honest assessment of himself, he had declared to Prince Bülow: 'Everything in me dislikes the thought of the appointment. I do not lack personal courage but I lack the power of rapid decision; I am too reflective; too scrupulous, or, if you like, too conscientious for such a post. I lack the capacity for risking all on a single throw'.[8] He, like all his predecessors, had to reassess Germany's overall strategic position in the light of changing circumstances and, as fate would have it, these changes pushed him in the more cautious direction that he naturally aspired to. The forces in the East were increased because the Russian railway system was improving rapidly with an influx of French capital and her mobilisation and forward deployment might be that much more efficient. He also gained some knowledge of the French intention to launch an immediate offensive into Alsace-Lorraine and so he increased the deployment of German forces in the south considerably (from one-seventh of the total available to one-third). Ludendorff agreed with this alteration, which would tie down and, hopefully, defeat a large part of the French field army, provided the extra troops needed came from new formations and did not involve a reduction of the actual strength of the great march to outflank Paris.

At the age of 44, this man, who so clearly revelled in the monastic life of the General Staff officer, suddenly revealed a romantic side to his character that few could have been aware of. Based on a purely chance meeting, and the gallant offering to share an umbrella with a lady caught out in a heavy rainfall, Ludendorff fell in love with the darkly attractive Frau Margarethe Pernet – a woman married since she had left school and the mother of four children. Within the space of a few months in 1909 she divorced her husband and married Erich Ludendorff, which must have astounded his professional colleagues. Where once this behaviour would have been professional suicide, now it merely raised a few eyebrows (and, perhaps, a few doubts). Nearly half the brilliant officers working on the Great General Staff were non-noble; this was truly a career open to talent above all things. It was no longer necessary to marry into noble, military families to guarantee advancement. The marriage was very happy; the charming Margarethe was warmly accepted by Ludendorff's family; he treated the stepchildren as if they were his own. His wife quickly adapted to the realities of his work; he would receive large quantities of papers every day that required him to work long into the night.

Ludendorff moved into a period in his life when great things seemed to open up before him; a full colonel in 1911, acting well above his rank, and such a close confidant of Moltke that he was widely tipped to become his chief of operations on the outbreak of the 'inevitable' war. All this was to be shattered in the political wrangling over the necessary size of the German Army to carry out the Schlieffen Plan effectively.

The decade before 1914 was a succession of international crises (over German interference in Morocco in 1905 and 1911; Austria's annexation of Bosnia and Herzegovina in 1908), a naval arms race as Germany rapidly increased the size of her fleet, of alliance building and some extremely bellicose speeches and articles in which the Germans and Austrians saw themselves as the victims of Franco-Russian encirclement (egged on by 'perfidious Albion') and calculating when was the right time to make a pre-emptive strike against this sea of enemies. But while the German Navy grew apace, the German budget would not allow the army to expand at a rate it considered adequate to the task it faced. As an added problem the powerful Social Democratic Party in the Reichstag bitterly opposed increased military spending. However much we see Germany as a belligerent nation, it remains true that she only conscripted 50 per cent of the available male population (compared to 85 per cent in France). As Moltke, with Ludendorff firmly grasping his elbow, put in appeals for more men and formations he was repeatedly fobbed off with derisory numbers. At one stage in 1909 the war minister told the General Staff that they could only expect an increase of some 7,000 men per annum to the total strength of the army. When Moltke asked for 300,000 more men as an absolute minimum in 1911, the Reichstag voted him 10,000. The patience of Ludendorff wore thin.

During the Agadir crisis of mid 1911 he again insisted that the war plans required another three army corps immediately and another three by 1913–14. With no serious consideration apparently being given to this request by the War Ministry, Ludendorff tried to mobilise political support within the Reichstag. Via the retired General Keim he briefed the president of the ultra-nationalist Pan-German League, Heinrich Class, to begin agitating for the extra troops. The War Ministry reacted very angrily and Ludendorff earned a severe reprimand; the first serious blot on his career. As the Balkans crisis spread through 1912 and 1913 into a series of savage local wars the whole international situation deteriorated. Ludendorff assisted Moltke in preparing new requests for more troops and encouraged him to approach Imperial Chancellor Bethmann-Hollweg directly. The War Ministry again took violent exception to this by-passing of its authority and the Kaiser also expressed dissatisfaction with the importuning by the General Staff. A compromise increase was agreed in the Reichstag in April 1913, allowing about two-thirds of the extra troops requested. But in this battle between the General Staff and the War Ministry the axe fell on the career of Erich Ludendorff.

In January 1913 he was abruptly removed from the Great General

Staff and returned to regimental duty. He was posted to Düsseldorf to command the 39th (Lower Rhine) Fusilier Regiment, a long way from one of the fashionable Brandenburg regiments he would have liked. After nine years service at the heart of the German military machine, this was punishment indeed. His opponents in the row over army expansion were advanced, one of them even being ennobled in the process. Indeed he inadvertently saw a message about himself addressed to his divisional commander in which the Military Cabinet in Berlin said that here was a colonel that needed to be taught some discipline! Ludendorff became the perfect regimental commander, as one might have expected, but the drilling of recruits was hardly the best use of his great intellect. He rapidly brought his regiment to a peak of efficiency; discipline was combined with the development of initiative. The younger officers came to adore him. He treated the summer manoeuvres far more seriously than many others and conducted himself as if in a war situation, taking delight in spoiling the plans of one corps commander who wanted to make a picnic of the whole affair for his wealthy friends.

In April 1914 he was promoted to major general and given the command of an infantry brigade – the 85th, stationed at Strasbourg. During staff rides in May it was hinted that he might soon return to the General Staff, perhaps as quartermaster general. In June he enjoyed some leave with two stepsons home from their cadet schools; the third stepson was serving already with the 31st Infantry Regiment. On the 28 June 1914 the heir apparent to the throne of Austria-Hungary and his wife were shot and killed at Sarajevo. As the international situation deteriorated, Ludendorff read the situation correctly and, towards the end of July, ordered his wife and stepchildren home from a holiday in Switzerland. He ordered the boys back to their cadet school just as the telegram arrived with the letters 'D. K.' (*drohende kriegsgefahr* – imminent danger of war).

Ludendorff had worked for years perfecting the mobilisation of the German Army for just this moment. Now he had the satisfaction of seeing his careful planning swing into action as trains full of eager troops, their horses and equipment left at the rate of one every ten minutes for the front all across the German Empire. His personal orders named him as deputy chief of staff to General Karl von Bülow's Second Army and doubtless he was placed there because he had made a detailed study of the 'problem' of Liège. When Moltke altered the Schlieffen Plan in order to avoid violating Dutch neutrality, he placed greater strain on the First and Second Armies that now had to march and fight their way through the heavily fortified Belgian positions in and around Liège. Schlieffen's final note had highlighted the possibility of fatal delays occurring if Liège was not reduced quickly. As early as 1911 Ludendorff had sent staff officers to 'holiday' in the area to study this vital ten-mile gap between Holland and the Ardennes. Speed was of the essence; anything less than a lightning victory in the West condemned Germany to a war on two fronts she was unlikely to win in the long run.

A German demand for the right to march through Belgium was immediately rejected by King Albert, who appealed to Great Britain for help. When Chancellor Bethmann-Hollweg told the German Cabinet that he expected Britain to declare war, Admiral Alfred von Tirpitz reportedly exclaimed, 'All is lost then!' which gives one pause for thought about the nature of the gamble that Germany was embarking upon.

On reporting to the Second Army's headquarters at Aachen, Ludendorff was appointed as a representative of the army commander to General Otto von Emmich's mixed force of six brigades earmarked for the seizure of Liège ahead of the main forces of the First and Second Armies. He was to 'co-ordinate General Emmich's plans with General Bülow's probable dispositions'. (Bülow was at his headquarters at Hanover as the campaign opened.) This was a typical German Army appointment – a position with no real rank and no authority to issue orders; General Emmich had his own chief of staff, General Lauenstein, who was technically senior to Ludendorff. Thus Ludendorff was free to think independently and had the great moral authority of the

Great General Staff, but he could only advise the formation commander and had to carefully negotiate around the residual resentment of Prussian officers to the 'interference' of an outsider.

German cavalry patrols were soon pushing through Belgium and came under fire from some justifiably angry and admirably brave Belgian civilians. The Germans reacted savagely, shooting hostages and burning villages in a calculated use of terror to pacify the rear areas. Ludendorff, who never for a moment questioned the blatant violation of Belgian neutrality, gives us a highly Prussian piece of canting hypocrisy: 'For my part, I had taken the field with chivalrous and humane conceptions of warfare. The *franc-tireur* warfare was bound to disgust any soldier. My soldierly spirit suffered bitter disillusion'.[9]

Riding well forward with Emmich's infantry, Ludendorff saw Belgian resistance stiffen at Visé, some fifteen miles from Liège. Here the 49-year-old general came under enemy fire for the first time in his life – a test he passed to his personal satisfaction. He learnt a very important lesson early on about the tendency of new troops to send back panic-stricken messages. Having suggested that a cyclist company go forward to reconnoitre, he was shocked to hear soon after that the entire company had been ambushed and slaughtered in a village. With just two men accompanying him, Ludendorff courageously went forward to investigate and found the company busily engaged in clearing the village, which was being stiffly contested as a cover for the destruction by Belgian engineers of the Meuse bridges.

The Germans closed in on Liège, with its twelve mutually supporting perimeter forts, 400 guns, and a garrison of 4,500 men reinforced by nearly 30,000 men of the field army. The German infantry, working to excellent maps prepared well in advance, were to use dead ground to infiltrate between the forts, leaving them to be dealt with by a 'secret' weapon. Ludendorff was one of a handful of officers who knew about the super-heavy siege howitzers that would be the nemesis of even the most modern fortresses.

As the infantry pressed forward, Ludendorff saw young men all around him falling in increasing numbers; saw the difficulty of getting these well-drilled but inexperienced men of 1914 to do what was required of them to fulfil 'the Plan'. He occasionally took personal command of shaken troops and led them forward with boldness and commitment. He personally guided one brigade between the forts and got deep into the Belgian position, noting that ammunition was already in short supply. All the combatant armies in 1914 fired off far more ammunition than they had expected. Logistical problems were beginning to accrue after only a few days.

On the night of 6–7 August we get the first of Ludendorff's confessions that the nervous strain of conducting operations was a burden to him. Still he managed to make his way back to Emmich's headquarters and agree a plan to continue his infantry attack deep within the fortress zone. In the confusion of battle Ludendorff thought that a regiment of von Oven's brigade had seized the citadel and so, early on 7 August, he drove up to it in a commandeered car with only the brigade adjutant beside him. He stepped out into the active heart of the Belgian resistance. With a cool courage and boldness he hammered on the doors and, by force of will, compelled the surrender of several hundred defenders.

Thus is a national hero made – the very stuff of legend. The German press could not know that Belgium's General Leman had already ordered the field troops to quit the fortress zone. Emmich's six brigades had been drawn from five different army corps and, when prisoners started to come in from these diverse formations, Leman assumed he was massively outnumbered. Instead Ludendorff was hailed as the man of the hour, with the legend already being garnished with tales of him beating on the citadel doors with the hilt of his sword. In truth he had conducted himself with courage and tactical acumen in his first battle. The Kaiser bestowed upon him (and General Emmich) the *Pour le Mérite*, Prussia's highest decoration for gallantry.

He returned to Aachen and, in the four days it took to get the siege artillery forward, he resumed normal staff duties. He was back in the front line to witness the opening bombardment of the Liège forts (two of which had already fallen to infantry assault), and watched with satisfaction as, one by one, they were battered into submission. 'The Plan' seemed to be unfolding smoothly. Brussels fell on 19 August. On 21 August Ludendorff saw the 2nd Guards Division of the Second Army cross the Sambre west of Namur. Next day he was moving with Bülow's headquarters between Wavre and Namur when a letter reached him from his old chief, Moltke, ordering him to a new posting in the East.

In East Prussia the Russians had advanced sooner than expected, and after border clashes the German Eighth Army was forced back. This was in accordance with German planning but the army commander seems to have panicked and his momentary loss of nerve sealed his fate.

The leadership of the Eighth Army was to be replaced and Moltke had immediately thought of Ludendorff as the new chief of staff. He wrote to him:

> You have before you a new and difficult task, perhaps even more difficult than the storming of Liège ... I know no other man in whom I have such absolute trust. You may yet be able to save the situation in the east. You must not be angry with me for calling you away from a post in which you are, perhaps, on the threshold of a decisive action, which, please God, will be conclusive. This is yet another sacrifice you are called upon to make for the Fatherland. The Kaiser, too, has confidence in you. Of course, you will not be made responsible for what has happened already, but with your energy you can prevent the worst from happening. So answer this new call, which is the greatest compliment that can be paid any soldier. I know that you will not belie the trust reposed in you.[10]

The quartermaster general, Stein, also wrote at the same time: 'You must go, therefore. The interests of the State make it imperative. Your task is a difficult one, but you are equal to it'. Ludendorff was told that General Paul von Beneckendorff und von Hindenburg had been offered command of the Eighth Army; apparently a relation of his on the Great General Staff remembered that he lived at Hanover, which that was conveniently on the railway route to the East. Before Hindenburg had replied Ludendorff had flung his few bits of kit into a staff car and set off for Coblenz and Imperial Headquarters. He later wrote:

> I was proud of my new task and of the trust placed in me. I was exalted at the thought of serving my Emperor, Army and Fatherland, in a position of greater responsibility at a most critical point ... No soldier could have had a better chance given him. But I was distressed that my appointment was the outcome of such a serious situation for my country.[11]

By 6 p.m. on 22 August he had joined Moltke at Coblenz for a thorough briefing on the crisis in East Prussia. He made a rapid assessment of the situation and began formulating a plan. At 8 p.m. he was invested with the *Pour le Mérite* by the Kaiser himself. By 9 p.m. he was aboard the train bound for Hanover and the East.

On the afternoon of 22 August Hindenburg received a telegram at his Hanover apartment from Imperial Headquarters at Coblenz asking if he was ready for immediate service (wholly unspecified at that time). He fired back a two-word reply: 'Am ready'. Later that day he was informed that he was the new general officer commanding the Eighth Army and that he was to join the train carrying his chief of staff, Ludendorff, early the next day. Hindenburg squeezed into his old Prussian blue uniform and was on the platform with his wife as the train steamed in at 4 a.m. on 23 August.

A remarkable four-year partnership was about to begin.

*chapter three*

# Campaigning in the East

The German Eighth Army in East Prussia understood its mission perfectly well. It was to delay the deployment of the First and Second Russian Armies for as long as possible and then conduct a fighting retreat to the line of the Vistula fortresses. That this would eventually entail the abandonment of parts of old Prussia to the hated 'Cossacks' was a strategic necessity. All would be redeemed when France was knocked out of the war and reinforcements could stream eastwards to settle accounts with the tsar.

It was known that the two Russian armies were advancing separately: General Pavel Rennenkampf's First Army was deployed along the Niemen River and General Alexander Samsonov's Second Army was still in Poland south of the Masurian Lakes. Russian cavalry (Gourko's 1st Division) entered German territory on 12 August 1914. The Eighth Army's commander, General Maximilian von Prittwitz, intended to engage Rennenkampf along the line of the Rominte but his I Corps commander, General Hermann von Francois was one of those highly combative and independent generals who couldn't bear the thought of Russian troops on German soil. He refused to fall back and clashed with Rennenkampf's infantry on 17 August at Stalluponen, inflicting 3,000 casualties before obeying Prittwitz's telegraphed orders

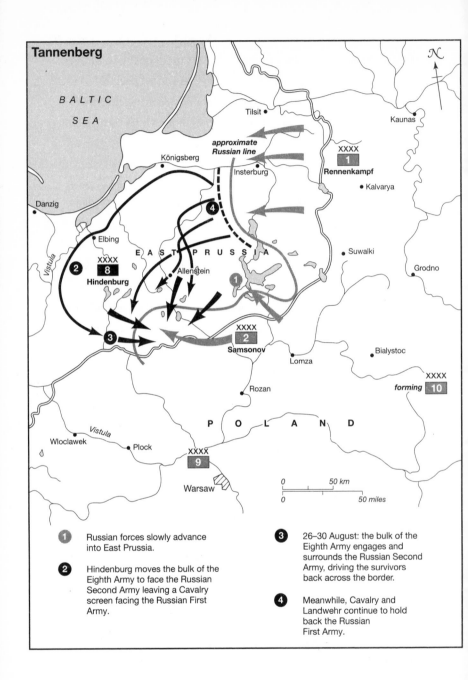

# Tannenberg

BALTIC
SEA

Tilsit •

Kaunas •

*approximate
Russian line*

XXXX
**1**
**Rennenkampf**

Königsberg •

Insterburg •

• Kalvarya

Danzig •

**4**

Elbing •

E A S T   P R U S S I A

XXXX
**8**
**Hindenburg**

**2**

Allenstein •

• Suwalki

Grodno •

**1**

XXXX
**2**
**Samsonov**

**3**

Lomza •

• Bialystoc

XXXX
*forming* **10**

Rozan •

P   O   L   A   N   D

Vistula

Wloclawek •

• Plock

XXXX
**9**

Warsaw •

| 0 | | 50 km |
| 0 | | 50 miles |

1. Russian forces slowly advance into East Prussia.

2. Hindenburg moves the bulk of the Eighth Army to face the Russian Second Army leaving a Cavalry screen facing the Russian First Army.

3. 26–30 August: the bulk of the Eighth Army engages and surrounds the Russian Second Army, driving the survivors back across the border.

4. Meanwhile, Cavalry and Landwehr continue to hold back the Russian First Army.

to rejoin the main army on the Rominte. On 20 August three German corps lashed out at the Russian First Army at Gumbinnen, driving its wings back in disorder but with August von Mackensen's XVII Corps suffering a sharp defeat in the centre. Next day the Germans broke contact and pulled back to lick their wounds.

Then Prittwitz momentarily lost his nerve. He heard that Samsonov's unopposed Second Army had marched through Ostrolenka and was well placed to cut the German Army off from the Vistula. When Prittwitz ordered an immediate retreat behind the line of the Vistula his staff, led by the brilliant Lieutenant Colonel Max Hoffmann, protested that the Gumbinnen 'victory' could be pressed with decisive results. Prittwitz was adamant and made the crucial error of making a deeply pessimistic phone call to Moltke at Coblenz. During the conversation he announced not only the complete abandonment of East Prussia but also expressed doubts about his ability to hold the Vistula. The prospect of Russians advancing on Berlin brought back images of the most humiliating episodes of the Seven Years' War.

Though his staff remained resolute and Prittwitz actually cancelled the order for a precipitate retreat, the damage was done. From Coblenz Moltke spoke by telephone to some Eastern corps commanders, including the fiery Francois, and determined to replace both Prittwitz and his chief of staff, Count von Waldersee. Ludendorff was his immediate choice for the staff; Hindenburg was a suitably senior general for the Eighth Army who was available for immediate service.

On 22 August Lieutenant Colonel Hoffmann and the staff of the Eighth Army had already determined to leave a light holding force before Rennenkampf's shaken army and concentrate all available forces against Samsonov to the south. Many miles away to the west, working only from maps and the situation reports at hand, Ludendorff arrived at exactly the same conclusions. He issued a stream of orders to the corps of the Eighth Army, concentrating them somewhat further south and east than Hoffmann, more ready for an immediate strike at the

Russian Second Army. This was a perfect example of Great General Staff thinking. Hoffmann and Ludendorff had roomed together in Berlin; it was entirely proper that their identical rigorous training should produce such similar conclusions about the need to screen one enemy force in order to concentrate everything against the other. As Ludendorff wrote, 'No staff officer would miss such a chance of turning to good advantage the fact that their two armies were separated'. It should also be remembered that in 1891, 1898 and 1899 the East Prussian manoeuvres had all revolved around the problem of multiple invasions by Russian forces and all had been resolved by just such a measure.

It was also entirely in keeping with the Prussian system that Ludendorff should act independently to order the necessary movements before he had actually met his new army commander. Within minutes of their meeting on the train at Hanover, Ludendorff had explained the situation and Hindenburg, accepting all the responsibility, endorsed the plan to the last detail. Margarethe Ludendorff joined the train from Berlin to Küstrin and records how, on first meeting Hindenburg, 'my heart went out to him in confidence and admiration'.[1] This was to be the abiding strength of the commander-in-chief, a calmness and sense of purpose that inspired all around him.

This calming influence was greatly needed at the Eighth Army's new headquarters at Marienburg. The staff there, headed by Hoffmann and the Quartermaster General Grunert, resented the sudden change in command and the way Ludendorff had by-passed army headquarters and sent orders direct to the corps commanders. Hindenburg's benign character immediately went some way to calming the situation as he addressed his new colleagues in terms of trusting each other and doing their duty together.

Rennenkampf's First Army was marking time to allow Samsonov to get into the German rear. It was, in any case, badly disorganised with its supply lines in very bad shape. To add to this inertia, the front commander, Zhilinsky, ordered Rennenkampf to begin preparations for the siege of Königsberg. Samsonov's Second Army had marched long and hard to come into action. Its troops were exhausted; its supply trains were falling far behind; heat, tiredness, hunger and thirst were degrading some otherwise perfectly good formations. The army was spread over some very wide and difficult country; more than dispatch riders could easily cover. Hence the large-scale reliance on radio communication, and the excessive use of *en clair* messages because of the low level of expertise in coding and decoding amongst the Russian staffs. The Germans famously listened in to a number of important messages that enabled them to take risks that might otherwise have seemed foolhardy. Since their basic plan did not depend entirely on these intercepts, their importance should not be exaggerated. It should be said that Samsonov did not have the best of relations with his chief of staff, Postovsky, but we must dismiss the idiotic story that he and Rennenkampf refused to co-operate because they had come to physical blows at Mukden railway station in 1905.

As Lieutenant General Scholtz's reinforced XX Corps began to absorb the first attacks by Samsonov's army on 23 August, the railway section of the Eighth Army's General Staff began its decisive role in the redeploying of the German formations facing Rennenkampf. Garrison troops from Königsberg covered the front as the whole of Francois's I Corps marched back to the railroad, entrained and moved right round to detrain at Deutsch Eylau behind the right flank of the XX Corps. From there they would develop the attack on Samsonov's exposed left wing. Ludendorff would have liked to deploy them even further south to drive deep into the Russian rear but there simply were not enough troops available to take the chance. The heirs of Schlieffen would have to be satisfied with surrounding part of the Russian Army, not all of it. The railway section did not have an easy time arranging things. Extra rolling stock had to come up from beyond the Vistula; a small flood caused delays. Personnel had to be reallocated to the work;

the movements were across the lateral lines of communications of the Eighth Army and had to be worked out in fine detail. It all took longer than might have been hoped. Next the 3rd Reserve Division was moved by rail to Allenstein to bolster the German centre; a move completed in forty-eight hours. Mackensen's XVII Corps was ordered south by road to descend upon the Russian's open right flank. Finally, Otto von Below's I Reserve Corps was ordered south to complete the envelopment of the Russian right. At that stage only the three brigades of the 1st Cavalry Division were left to face the combined, but mercifully passive, might of Rennenkampf's First Army.

Hindenburg and Ludendorff, having set everything in motion, were quite happy to let the Eighth Army staff get on with the routine running of the army. They were very active in visiting corps headquarters to see how things progressed at the front and to offer support and advice. On 24 August they visited the XX Corps in the pretty little village of Tannenberg. Hindenburg later wrote that he liked what he saw as Scholtz's staff seemed calm and in good spirits; the more nervous Ludendorff was already urging them to 'hold on to the last man' to buy time for Francois to deploy by 26 August. The following day saw them at Francois's I Corps headquarters to finalise details for the enveloping attack the next day. Argumentative as ever, Francois explained that his artillery would not be in place in time and that he could not attack until 27 August. Ludendorff grew very angry and threatened to have him replaced; Hindenburg had worked with Francois before the war and his old chief's ominous silence on the matter was enough to make him come into line, with assurances that headquarters would do everything they could to speed up his artillery and reinforcements. That evening they received confirmation that Rennenkampf was not moving into their rear, and also that a Landwehr division was on its way to reinforce them. Hindenburg, Ludendorff and Hoffmann were quietly confident that their bold manoeuvre would yield good results. It was entirely in character for Ludendorff to be too nervous for sleep, and for

Hindenburg to announce, 'Gentlemen, our preparations are so well in hand that we can sleep soundly tonight'.[2] And he did!

Wednesday, 26 August was a day to test their nerves to the limit. To begin with Francois did not open his attack at the time ordered, though he blatantly deceived the Eighth Army into thinking that he had. He absolutely refused to throw his men at well-prepared Russian positions without a proper artillery bombardment. Under the furious onslaught of an irate Ludendorff, who would have sacked him if there had been anyone remotely capable of replacing him at short notice, Francois opened his attack late and finished it early, for his ill-supported infantry really did run into ferocious resistance. This sort of insubordination was 'permitted' under the German military system, where the field commander was given a broad 'mission statement' and was free to work out the detail of its execution. Francois was pushing the limits of his commander's patience and it is fortunate for him that later studies of the battle showed that he was right to delay his attack. Another commander would personally reinterpret his orders that day and fortuitously do the right thing. The 3rd Reserve Division had been ordered forward to support an attack by the XX Corps but its commander felt that he was in danger of running into powerful Russian forces in the area. By an intelligent reading of the local situation and having the moral courage to 'disobey', he saved his division from the embrace of an entire Russian corps. The XX Corps had shown just how flexible German troops could be when they switched from a fighting withdrawal into a swift riposte on receiving good local intelligence of a wide gap opening between the Russian formations moving against them. Their spirited counter-attack destroyed the Russian 2nd Division as an effective unit. More importantly, the XVII and I Reserve Corps successfully attacked the Russians around Bischofsburg and drove first their 16th Division and then the whole of their VI Corps from the field completely. In these fierce encounter battles Below's reservists showed themselves to be every bit as good as Mackensen's 'active' divisions.

But things did not look good at the Eighth Army headquarters that night. The disappointment of the I Corps' lack of progress was compounded by news that units of the Russian Imperial Guard had been identified coming up from the south (it was actually only one division coming up as a reinforcement) but the threat to the Eighth Army's open right flank was potentially serious. Then a rumour (false as it turned out to be) that Rennenkampf might be on the move made it look as if it was the German Army about to be surrounded and annihilated. During an evening meal eaten in dead silence, Ludendorff furiously rolled his bread about the table; a sign to all who knew him that he was either deeply concentrating or was deeply worried. He suddenly leaped to his feet and asked Hindenburg if he could see him privately. There can be no doubt that at this critical moment it took all Hindenburg's calm and passive nature to keep the highly-strung Ludendorff from changing the plan to meet these new crises. In the best traditions of the army commander, Hindenburg shouldered all the responsibility for whatever might come to pass, and encouraged his brilliant chief of staff to carry through their bold conception.

Ludendorff issued a set of calm and well-measured orders for the next day's fighting, as the whole German Army began to put Samsonov's men under greater and greater pressure. The I Corps, well-rested and fully-assembled, stormed Usdau after some hard fighting. Although they put one German brigade to flight, the Russian I Corps was so shaken by this unexpected attack that it fled the field in disorder. In a day of very hard fighting the XX Corps absorbed attacks by Russia's XV Corps and forced them over to the defensive. Hindenburg and Ludendorff spent the morning with Scholtz to stiffen his resolve. An alarming development was the debouching from the woods of an entire Russian corps (the XIII) into the town of Allenstein, deep in the German rear. The railway section of the army staff, already engaged in moving army headquarters up to Osterode, was expecting to detrain there the Landwehr division which had been dispatched from the Danish border to reinforce the Eighth Army. After a gallant personal reconnaissance by a staff lieutenant, who rode a train almost into Allenstein, within two hours the reinforcements were rerouted to Biessellen, where they were well placed to cover the centre. The XVII and I Reserve Corps were beginning to exploit their success of the previous day towards the south; initially the Russians were running faster than the Germans could chase them. By evening they, along with army headquarters, had received the bad news from in and around Allenstein. It was Below who suggested that both his and Mackensen's corps should turn upon these Russians the next day (28 August) and drive them into the arms of the XX Corps, 3rd Reserve Division and the newly-arrived Landwehr. The Eighth Army approved the plan immediately.

This change did involve a good deal of confusion, with one corps receiving orders to press south and turn back on Allenstein at the same time. Tiredness was setting in; the stress and strain of constant action was beginning to tell on these men. Meanwhile Samsonov, still ignorant of the fact that he faced the whole of Germany's Eighth Army, was making what he thought were good orders for concentrating the whole of his XIII and XV Corps to break the German centre. He personally went forward to the XV Corps headquarters to direct the action. He was delivering two corps into a German noose tightening around them.

Friday, 28 August was another topsy-turvy day. The XX Corps' attacks did not fare well with 'active' divisions performing badly (admittedly hampered by thick fog and a counterstroke by Russia's XV Corps). There were even large-scale German surrenders to a still aggressive enemy. Yet on their left the reserve and Landwehr formations of von Morgen and Baron von der Goltz did much better in equally stiff fighting, until halted by news that the Russians from Allenstein were in their rear. On the right the I Corps began its pursuit of the beaten Russians before them. When he received orders to swing his divisions inwards towards the north-east to rescue the XX Corps from supposed disaster, Francois instinctively knew it was the wrong thing to do. He covered himself from yet another charge of disobedience by halting one of his divisions, to feed, rest and be ready for any further deployment necessary, but urged his other division and its attached reinforcements (Schmettau's force, drawn largely from the XX Corps) to plunge on towards Neidenburg, deep in the Russian rear. At 4 p.m. and leading from the front, Francois and his personal staff got into a firefight as their forward troops burst into the town as the Russians were leaving in haste. The Russians began to surrender in thousands. In the northern sector of the battlefield some friction was setting in between the commanders of the I Reserve Corps and the XVII Corps. Below gave his men a rest before attacking the Russians now known to be evacuating Allenstein in a hurry; Mackensen, tired of marching and countermarching, was ordering Below off the road and out of his way so he could get at the retreating enemy. At the least an appalling traffic jam threatened to halt all operations. The Eighth Army recognised that it had made a serious error in directing both corps towards Allenstein and now ordered the XVII Corps to strike south with all speed, leaving Below to 'liberate' Allenstein and fall upon the baggage trains of the retreating Russian XIII Corps. The Russian formations began to disintegrate as they fled but their rearguards put up fierce resistance.

Once again, towards the end of 28 August, a report of Rennenkampf's forward movement threw Ludendorff into a near panic. He began to talk of abandoning the fight with Samsonov to meet Rennenkampf. Again Hindenburg took him aside, spoke to him quietly in private and returned to order the operations to proceed at full pace to complete the impending victory. It was about this time that Ludendorff began dictating a dispatch announcing their success to General Headquarters, which was to be sent from Frogenau. Hoffmann noticed that the next village was Tannenberg and suggested using it as a name for the battle, reversing the disastrous defeat of the Teutonic Knights by the Slavs some five hundred years before. A cheerful Hindenburg wanted to visit the front lines of the XX Corps to thank the men personally for their great efforts. That the staff convoy was caught up in one of those rear area panics that see columns of prisoners as a new enemy threat shows just what a strain all elements of the German Army were under in this continuous fighting.

The next day, 29 August, saw the Russian Army driven into an ever tightening pocket and descending into chaos in the process. The I Corps sealed the southern rim and fought all day against Russians trying to break out to freedom. Schmettau's force was especially vigorous in this final stage of the fighting. The XVII and I Reserve Corps were still pushing south against stiff resistance and were themselves in some disorder. Hindenburg began to insist personally that his orders for the day be followed to the letter. Both he and his chief of staff could see Russians slipping out of their grasp; Ludendorff was already drafting dispatches that would blame the failures of some corps commanders for the less than total victory that was unfolding. It was Below who now played the rebel and ignored an army order to send half his corps off to the south-east, when he had his hands full with fighting towards the south. Ludendorff started to stand down some of the divisions in the centre and redeploy them to face Rennenkampf (who was actually moving troops off towards Königsberg at that time). The official tally of prisoners passed the 10,000 mark; Hindenburg officially asked the Kaiser to accept the name Tannenberg for the battle. (It was at this time that the commander dropped 'Beneckendorff' and began signing himself 'Hindenburg').

Sometime during the night of 29–30 August Samsonov accepted that he had completely failed to control the battle, had led his army to utter defeat and he preferred death by suicide to facing the disgrace. Lost in swampy woodland, with only his personal staff about him, and with German troops closing in all around, he slipped quietly away at midnight and shot himself. During 30 August elements of the I Corps had to fight off a serious attack from the south, while all across the battlefield the Russians of the shattered central corps surrendered in vast numbers. By 31 August the prisoners numbered 92,000; 300 guns were captured. Other casualties may have exceeded 50,000. Russia's Second Army, though not annihilated, was no longer a force to be reckoned with.

Rennenkampf's First Army was. At the height of the recent fighting Ludendorff had been surprised to receive a call from Moltke offering substantial reinforcements to the Eighth Army. The fall of fortress Namur in Belgium had released two corps for service elsewhere and, with things going so well on the Western Front in August, Moltke wanted to send them, with a cavalry division, to East Prussia. Ludendorff bluntly said they were not required as the battle was going to plan and he, as a firm believer in Schlieffen's plan, did not want to see the West losing troops that might be needed for the decisive battle. Still the XI and I Guards Reserve Corps were on their way and the Eighth Army's staff began immediately to plan for their deployment to settle accounts with Rennenkampf.

The Russian forces were well rested and had dug some strong defensive positions. They were also being reinforced on their left by a newly and somewhat hastily assembled Russian Tenth Army. Leaving light covering forces to clear up the southern battlefield, the Eighth Army's staff, and especially its tireless railway section, ordered a fairly complex redeployment out of one battle area and straight into the attack positions of the next one. From south to north they deployed the I and XVII Corps, to serve as the main assault formations of a new encirclement battle. Then came the XX, XI, I Reserve and Guards Reserve Corps. A general attack began on 7 September.

The I Corps struck the newly arrived XXII (Finnish) Corps of Flug's Tenth Army and, with a local superiority of four to one, routed it completely, inflicting heavy losses. The XVII Corps however ran into a very stubborn Russian defence and suffered severely. All along the line the Germans closed with a determined enemy. Francois continued his drive into the Russian rear and reached Lyck, effectively turning

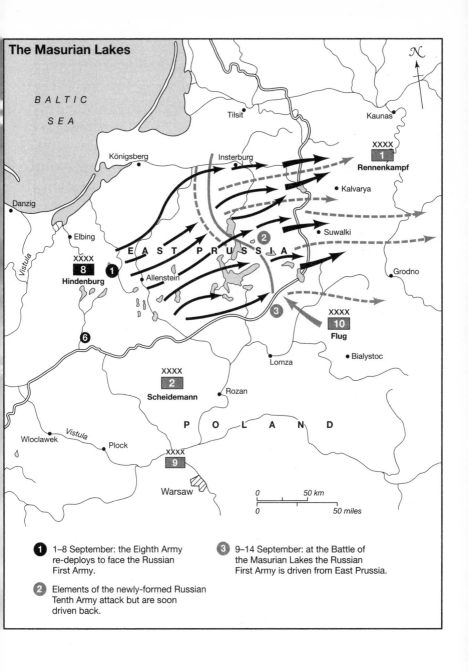

# The Masurian Lakes

BALTIC
SEA

Tilsit

Kaunas

Königsberg

Insterburg

XXXX
1
**Rennenkampf**

Kalvarya

Danzig

Elbing

XXXX
8
**Hindenburg**

E A S T   P R U S S I A

2

Suwalki

Grodno

Allenstein

3

XXXX
10
**Flug**

6

Bialystoc

Lomza

XXXX
2
**Scheidemann**

Rozan

P O L A N D

Wloclawek

Vistula

Plock

XXXX
9

Warsaw

0        50 km
0              50 miles

**1** 1–8 September: the Eighth Army
re-deploys to face the Russian
First Army.

**3** 9–14 September: at the Battle of
the Masurian Lakes the Russian
First Army is driven from East Prussia.

**2** Elements of the newly-formed Russian
Tenth Army attack but are soon
driven back.

Rennenkampf's left. The 1st Division of the I Corps had the extraordinary advantage of fighting over its old peacetime training grounds. The Russians began a measured withdrawal; their XX Corps on the extreme right was to occupy a 'fall back' position covering Gumbinnen. But by 9 September Francois had switched his line of attack to the north and broke into the flank of the Russian's holding up Mackensen's XVII Corps. Together these two veteran formations put the Russian left to flight and they expected to roll up the entire Russian line and create another stunning encirclement victory.

The Russian Army saved itself from disaster by, quite simply, running away as fast as the legs of men and horses could carry them. Retreating at a rate of twenty-five miles a day, they left their exhausted German pursuers far behind. They lost most of their artillery, all their transport and large numbers of prisoners but the bulk of the fighting troops escaped to fight another day. The battle of the Masurian Lakes was another clear, if incomplete, victory. Germany's Eighth Army under its new and relatively unknown leaders, had liberated all German soil from the invader.

How the German people adored the victor, Hindenburg. His massive frame exuded a calm authority; he was religious, modest and silent, devoid of ambition and anxious only to serve his Kaiser, his Saviour and his Fatherland. He was one of the heroes of the wars of liberation and unification come to save his people in their hour of need. It must be recognised that the Hindenburg legend, which would have taken root anyway, was enormously enhanced because the war was going horribly wrong everywhere else. Just days after Moltke had confidently offered and sent reinforcements from the West to the East, the shocking defeat on the Marne had sent the German armies reeling back from the very gates of Paris. Just as the Russian armies were chased from East Prussia they smashed the Austrian field armies in Galicia and drove them back to the line of the Carpathian Mountains, from where they threatened to invade Silesia and Hungary. The high hopes and the great gamble of the short, violent but victorious 'war by railway timetable' lay in ruins; the dreadful prospect of a long war against numerous and implacable enemies had become a reality.

The German press fanned the flames of the idolisation of Hindenburg. The wholly fictitious story of his having, in his retirement, borrowed troops and guns from the Königsberg garrison to plan defensive battles in and around the Masurian Lakes soon appeared and no amount of denials could gainsay it. The name of Hindenburg was everywhere as streets and squares were renamed after him, as were restaurant dishes and wines. Letters poured in from admirers; he was the new talisman for an anxious nation and he eclipsed the Kaiser in the popular imagination. None of this adulation embraced Erich Ludendorff, unless he was referred to as the faithful assistant and loyal comrade of the great chief. This suited the Spartan character of the consummate staff officer; as long as his professional colleagues recognised his important role, he seemed content to stand in the shadow of his commander.

Now was to begin a long and increasingly acrimonious debate about where Germany should make her main effort, and where new formations and precious reserves of men and *matériel* should be committed to force a military decision significant enough to advance the Reich's admittedly vague war aims. By 14 September Moltke had been 'invalided' and, without any announcement to the outside world, he was replaced as Chief of the General Staff of the Army in the Field by the Prussian War Minister Lieutenant General Erich von Falkenhayn, at 52 the youngest ever holder of that important post. He was firmly committed to seeking victory on the Western Front against the main enemies, France and Great Britain. The new corps of war volunteers, formed in August 1914 from the excellent young enthusiasts who didn't want to wait to be called up, were sent to Flanders where the continual reaching around the only open flank left to exploit by either protagonist, the so-called 'race to the sea', ended in the bloody First

Battle of Ypres, where the professional soldiers of the British Expeditionary Force inflicted the most appalling losses on the keen but untried youth of Germany.

Naturally enough the victors of Tannenberg and the Masurian Lakes stood ready to exploit their success. General Headquarters ordered the creation of a new Ninth Army from the formations of the enlarged Eighth Army. It was to deploy the XI, XVII, XX and Guards Reserve Corps, the 35th Reserve Division and two cavalry divisions southwards by train to Upper Silesia for operations against the Russians in Poland; Hindenburg was to be its commander, with Ludendorff as his chief of staff and Hoffmann as chief of operations. During this redeployment Ludendorff had first to cope with the news that his eldest stepson, Franz, had been seriously wounded in France. He was invalided out of the infantry with the Iron Cross, but recovered well and received his stepfather's blessing to transfer to the air force. Ludendorff also made an important visit to the Austro-Hungarian headquarters, where he established good relations with their chief of staff, Conrad von Hötzendorf, and agreed to launch an offensive towards Warsaw to take pressure off the Austrians in the south. It was during this trip that he memorably heard of the conversation between one of his staff officers and a 'Jew in Radom' who wondered why a strong and vital nation like Germany had allied itself to a corpse like Austria-Hungary. With the wisdom of hindsight in his post-war memoirs Ludendorff concluded sardonically, 'He was right'.

The Ninth Army attacked on 29 September and made good initial progress towards Warsaw, hampered by poor weather and primitive roads. A large part of the intricate staff work going into the operation was to do with repairing roads and railways, converting Russian broad gauge track to European standard gauge and constructing new branch lines and bridges. What could not be overcome was the simple fact that the Russians were pouring hundreds of thousands of fresh troops into Poland – four armies in all. In a savage fight between the XVII Corps and some Siberian troops on 9 October the Germans had the good fortune to find details of the Russian order of battle on the dead body of a Russian officer. Hindenburg and Ludendorff realised that their eighteen worn divisions were facing sixty fresh Russian divisions. Out of loyalty to their Austrian allies, who had launched an offensive with three armies on 4 October, the Germans kept up their attacks, though they were pushing into ever increasing danger of being overwhelmed. A pattern was developing of Hindenburg and Ludendorff appealing for reinforcements from General Headquarters, and for Falkenhayn to turn down the request peremptorily. The Austrian offensive relieved the siege of Przemysl but did not develop further. Then Conrad, having taken over a section of the line along the Vistula, tried a clever stratagem of abandoning his defences to entice the Russians over the river and render themselves vulnerable to a counter-attack. It might have worked with veteran German troops but against demoralised Austrians the Russians simply crashed through and forced a general retreat of Germans and Austrians alike. The Ninth Army conducted such a well-organised retreat, and did such extensive damage to roads and railways as they fell back, that the Russians ground to a halt as they moved away from their own railheads. If the first attempt to take pressure off the Austrians had come to nothing, Ludendorff had no intention of surrendering the initiative for long.

By another remarkable use of the railway as a 'force multiplier' Ludendorff and his staff, now serving Hindenburg in his capacity as commander-in-chief of all German forces in the East, moved Mackensen's Ninth Army north in just five days to the area around Thorn. Radio intercepts had revealed the Russian plan to invade East Prussia again with their Second and Fifth Armies. Both sides began their attack on 11 November. The Germans struck the exposed flank of Scheidemann's Second Army and immediately halted it. Scheidemann promptly fell back on Lodz, his main supply base, maintaining close contact with Plehve's Fifth Army on his left. As the Germans thought they were closing in for the kill on a beaten enemy, they suddenly found themselves involved in desperate fighting at the end of fragile supply lines. As the combative Plehve hurried his troops into the battle, and Rennenkampf's First Army descended from the north, it was German formations that found themselves surrounded and facing annihilation. The day was saved by the extraordinary achievement of General Scheffer-Boydell, who fought his XXV Reserve Corps and the 3rd Guards Division and a cavalry corps attached, out of the trap. In a display of courage and heroism as fine as any in military history, they not only scattered the Russians surrounding them but conducted a fighting retreat back to their own lines bringing 16,000 prisoners with them. Another major threat to East Prussia had been ended, the Russians had been severely mauled (though German losses were nearly as great after a failed attempt to renew their own offensive) and the Hindenburg–Ludendorff team again announced another 'crushing' victory in the East. However incomplete the victory might have been it was still a remarkable display of strong nerves by the German commanders, and expertise by the railway section of the General Staff. Effectively they turned the German Ninth Army into a 'fire brigade' that disrupted the offensive plans of seven Russian field armies. Hindenburg was made a field marshal; Ludendorff was promoted to lieutenant general.

Despite the battle of Lodz being an incomplete victory, it greatly fuelled the increasingly acrimonious fight between those convinced that reinforcements should go east to finish with the Russians, and those who understood that the main enemy stood on the Western Front. Falkenhayn also recognised that the German Army needed to recover over the winter from the terrible losses it had suffered. All divisions in the field were reduced in size (but not in equivalent firepower) to free up veteran units to act as the cadres for new divisions and army corps. The split ran through the army and the government. The Foreign Office sought yet another approach, in that it favoured helping Austria-Hungary defeat Serbia and open up the lines of communication with their Turkish

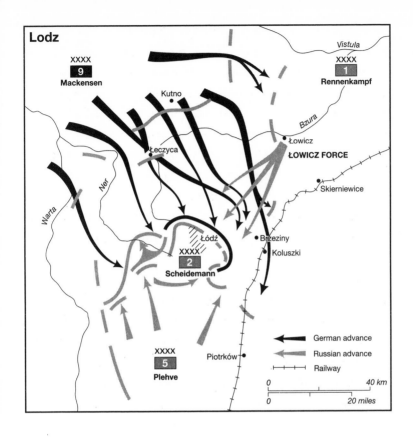

# Lodz

| XXXX | |
|---|---|
| **9** | |
| **Mackensen** | |

Kutno

Łeczyca

| XXXX | |
|---|---|
| **1** | |
| **Rennenkampf** | |

*Vistula*

*Bzura*

Łowicz

**ŁOWICZ FORCE**

Skierniewice

Łódź

| XXXX | |
|---|---|
| **2** | |
| **Scheidemann** | |

Brzeziny

Koluszki

*Warta*

*Ner*

| XXXX | |
|---|---|
| **5** | |
| **Plehve** | |

Piotrków

| | |
|---|---|
| ⬅ | German advance |
| ⬅ | Russian advance |
| ├┼┼┼┤ | Railway |

| 0 | 40 km |
|---|---|
| 0 | 20 miles |

allies, influencing Bulgaria, Romania and possibly Greece along the way. Hindenburg gave his support to this idea as it was more 'Eastern' than 'Western', and would put more pressure on Russia. Chancellor Bethmann–Hollweg, looking for some kind of victory to relieve the gloomy stalemate in the West, was drawn into the anti-Falkenhayn camp.

He rather recklessly began lobbying the Kaiser for Falkenhayn to be replaced by Ludendorff. A letter of support for this scheme from the Crown Prince, serving as an army commander on the Western Front, only served to annoy the Kaiser still further. He thought Ludendorff was a dubious character devoured by personal ambition. His riposte was to confirm Falkenhayn in his post as chief of the General Staff, while relieving him of his duties as Prussian war minister. Hindenburg then weighed in with a demand for Falkenhayn's resignation, while the Eastern Command began the most blatant lobbying for an enhanced role for the Eastern Front by sending a staff major, Hans von Haeften, to push the idea at General Headquarters and even amongst the army commanders on the Western Front. Falkenhayn continued to oppose the idea of a general offensive in the depths of an Eastern winter. When Hindenburg sent several divisions from the Ninth Army to the south to help the Austrians, Falkenhayn had them organised into a German 'South Army' under General Alexander von Linsingen and mischievously ordered Ludendorff to join it as the chief of staff. No sooner had he left than Hindenburg demanded his return, under threat of his own resignation. The Kaiser would cheerfully have court-martialled the field marshal but his chancellor knew that an attack on the national hero would be political suicide. In the end Hindenburg got his chief of staff back, and four new corps as reinforcements for a new offensive in the East.

As yet another Austrian offensive broke down in the Carpathian Mountains in late January 1915, Hindenburg now deployed three armies (Below's Eighth, Mackensen's Ninth and Eichhorn's Tenth), 150,000 men in fifteen infantry and two cavalry divisions, for another 'battle of annihilation' to destroy Gurko's Russian Tenth Army by attacking either side of the Masurian Lakes. This was the classic period of shortages in the Russian Army when there were more men than rifles available; reinforcements had to literally wait about for men to be killed or wounded before they could take up the rifles of the casualties to join the fray. In the most appalling weather, driving blizzards of snow, the two German wings drove forward, forcing an entire Russian corps to surrender in the Augustowo Forest. But they could not build up any momentum of advance to enable them to achieve the looked for encirclement. Though they would claim to have captured 110,000 men, the Germans actually took some 55,000 prisoners, with 185 guns. The second battle of the Masurian Lakes (7–12 February 1915) might have disappointed in its overall outcome but the German public saw that Hindenburg and his team had yet again delivered East Prussian territory from the clutches of the Slavic invader and the legend of invincibility just went on growing.

The Kaiser responded by awarding Hindenburg the coveted *Pour le Mérite*. It was at this time that the celebrated artist, Paul Vogel, joined the headquarters in the East to begin working on a series of portraits of the field marshal and his chief staff officers, and battle paintings of which the huge canvas portraying Tannenberg is the best known example, to satisfy the clamorous demands of the German people for more images of their hero and his 'band of brothers'. Hindenburg's critics take delight in pointing out the amount of time he spent in Vogel's studios and the extraordinary painstaking attention he gave to making sure that the tiniest detail of location and uniform were exactly as they should be. We should be sufficiently aware of the importance of war artists in sustaining home front morale, and of the mindset of professional soldiers and the important role of tradition in their lives, to discount a lot of this as carping criticism by people ill-informed concerning what helps men function in that most extreme and stress-inducing activity that is war. In similar vein, Hindenburg is also derided for the way he 'held court' at GHQ East to a constant stream

THE WARLORDS

of distinguished visitors, be they military, royal, political, industrial, financial or academic. Every commander-in-chief in every army had to conduct himself in a similar fashion. High command involved a great deal of playing the 'figurehead' while the staff officers got on with the minutiae of planning logistics and operations.

The mischievous Hoffmann was the source of many a story highlighting the extent to which Ludendorff (and himself) did most of the hard work at headquarters, while the commander took most of the credit. At this stage of the war Hoffmann wrote of Ludendorff as a 'first class fellow' and all three of them were adamant that Russia could be knocked out of the war if only they were given the reinforcements to put their large schemes into practice. While the soldiers recognised the truly formidable nature of the task facing them, and Hindenburg would privately warn against making too large a territorial demand in any likely peace talks, the German people and their political leaders could see German armed forces encamped everywhere on enemy territory and thought the war was going well. Wartime shortages and rationing were beginning to impact on their daily lives; the drive for home produced substitutes for pre-war imports now denied to them would see an increasingly awful range of 'ersatz' commodities that would eventually sap the health and resilience of the nation, but all that was in the future and, in the East, German forces went from victory to victory.

Falkenhayn openly despised the 'victory' of the second battle of the Masurian Lakes, where he saw his new formations used up for a narrow tactical success. He denied the possibility of annihilating the Russian forces because they were too numerous, his own forces were too stretched, and the Russians could retreat at their leisure into the empty wastes of their homeland and live to fight another day. When the besieged fortress of Przemysl was surrendered by the Austrians (with another 120,000 of them passing into captivity in March 1915), he saw with alarm that it released another three Russian corps to add to the threat on the Carpathian front. Having successfully withstood

72

two offensives on the Western Front (by the French in the Champagne and the British at Neuve-Chappelle, he decided to allow a major reinforcement of the Eastern Front for an offensive which he intended would destroy Russia's offensive capacity for that campaigning season. Ten veteran divisions and large quantities of artillery, including heavy batteries, were withdrawn from France and sent to the East.

But they would not go to the commander-in-chief in the East. Hindenburg was ordered to launch an offensive in the north, just as he had been requesting, but only as a diversion for much larger operations being planned for the south. In a bold and ingenious stroke, he launched what was effectively a massive cavalry raid into a region thinly garrisoned by the Russians. Seven cavalry and two infantry divisions burst over Lithuania and Courland and were soon threatening the important depot of Riga. Not least of their successes was that two Russian armies had to be moved up from the south into the area. Hindenburg's team were convinced they were on the brink of a decisive breakthrough into the Russian rear. Their demand for more troops fell on deaf ears.

Instead, eight divisions went to a new Eleventh Army to which the fiery Mackensen was appointed, with the brilliant Colonel Hans von Seeckt as his chief of staff. He was also given executive command of the Austrian Fourth Army, with both under the purely nominal high command of Conrad von Hötzendorf. They went into the line between the towns of Gorlice and Tarnow, just to the north of the Carpathian Mountains. On a front of twenty-eight miles, the heaviest artillery bombardment yet seen on the Eastern Front led to a brilliantly-executed attack on 2 May. The Russian Third Army collapsed, losing 140,000 prisoners in six days. Their Third and Eighth Armies were forced back to the San River. Fierce Russian counter-attacks merely added to their ruinous losses.

Disagreements as to what to do next came to a head at a series of meetings at General Headquarters (which had moved to Pless to oversee operations) in the summer of 1915. In June, at a meeting attended by the Kaiser, Ludendorff insisted that merely pushing the Russians back was a pointless exercise and that every operation should be designed to encircle and destroy them. Falkenhayn repeatedly denied that this was feasible in a theatre of war so enormous, against an enemy so numerous. He reminded those present that Italy had just declared war on Austria-Hungary and that Austrian troops would soon have to be redeployed from Galicia to the Italian front. He also expected a renewal of Allied attacks on the Western Front, and might need to send troops back to France. Ludendorff went ahead and planned a huge offensive operation that would carry Germany's northern armies past Kovno and Vilna and drive deep into the operational rear of the Russian armies. This plan was dismissed at the July conference because Mackensen's forces were still driving the Russians back in Galicia (where the prisoner tally had reached 240,000) and where mounting losses had eaten up all available reserves. Hoffmann reports that Ludendorff returned to GHQ East 'in a savage temper', made worse as Mackensen's armies went on to ever greater victories driving north-east towards the Russian border and threatening Warsaw from the south.

Falkenhayn sent his operations officer, Colonel Gerhard Tappen, to co-ordinate the attack by Hindenburg's forces to close in on Warsaw. He found Ludendorff arrogant and of a nervous disposition. The subsequent highly satisfactory attack owed much of its success to the careful planning of an artillery officer who deserves the title 'genius', Colonel Georg Bruchmuller. This artillery instructor, recalled to the colours from retirement (the British would have called him a 'dug out'), devised the most brilliant methods for using whatever guns he had to hand in the most devastatingly effective manner.

Further attacks due east forced a general retreat by the Russians. A daily exchange of argumentative cables between GHQ East and Falkenhayn at Pless fuelled the dispute over future operations. Ludendorff's temper was atrocious at this time; he was held to take every denial of reinforcement as a personal insult. Some feared for his mental health and he had to apologise at least once to Colonel Tappen, claiming that the strain of conducting such intensive operations with so few resources was affecting him badly.

The fall of Warsaw (5 August) was another propaganda triumph for Hindenburg but he still found that he was not invited to the Kaiser's triumphal entry into the recently surrendered Russian fortress of Novo-georgievsk. Hindenburg and Ludendorff attended anyway, were coldly received by their sovereign and got into further acrimonious words with Falkenhayn. Though the rate of advance slowed appreciably, Mackensen continued to drive the Russians back, capturing Brest-Litovsk and finally halting well inside Russia before getting embroiled in the Pripyet Marshes. Still the spectacular advance had not finished Russia as a threat. Early attempts to interest the tsar in a separate, nego-tiated peace had met with complete failure.

To stifle the enthusiasm of the Hindenburg team, Falkenhayn detached the Ninth Army and the Woyrsch Detachment from them to form the basis of a new army group under Prince Leopold of Bavaria. At the same time he placed the governance of conquered Poland under General Hans von Beseler, reporting not to the commander-in-chief in the East but directly to the Kaiser. Further threats to resign by Hindenburg and Ludendorff only added to the general acrimony amongst Germany's leaders. In September 1915, when Falkenhayn was trying to wind down Eastern operations in order to defend in the West and settle with Serbia once and for all, Hindenburg and Hötzendorf both continued attacking in the north and the south as part of their larger efforts to fight strategic battles of annihilation. Some further brilliant staff work saw twenty-eight infantry and five cavalry divisions rapidly concentrated on a sixty-five mile front in the north. The offensive captured Kovno, Grodno and Vilna before petering out in exhaustion in late September. The Austrians in the south faced further heavy losses in another dreary failure.

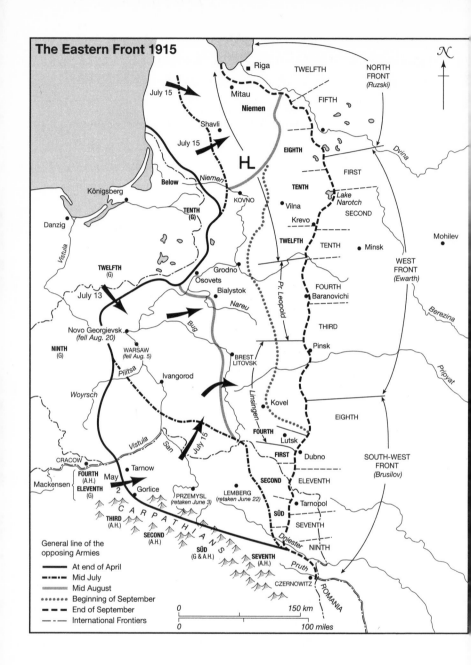

# The Eastern Front 1915

Riga
TWELFTH
NORTH FRONT (Ruzski)

July 15
Mitau
FIFTH

Niemen

Shavli
July 15

EIGHTH

Dvina

Below
Niemen
HL
TENTH (G)

Königsberg
KOVNO
FIRST

Danzig
Vilna
TENTH
Lake Narotch
SECOND

Krevo

Mohilev

Vistula

TWELFTH (G)
TWELFTH
TENTH
Minsk

WEST FRONT (Ewarth)

July 13
Grodno
Osovets
Bialystok

FOURTH
Baranovichi

Pr. Leopold

Nareu

Berezina

Novo Georgievsk (fell Aug. 20)
Bug

THIRD

NINTH (G)
WARSAW (fell Aug. 5)
Pilitsa
Ivangorod

BREST LITOVSK
Pinsk

Pripyat

Woyrsch

Linsingen
Kovel
EIGHTH

Vistula
San
July 15
FOURTH
Lutsk
SOUTH-WEST FRONT (Brusilov)

CRACOW
Tarnow
FIRST
Dubno

Mackensen
FOURTH (A.H.)
May 2
Gorlice
ELEVENTH (G)
PRZEMYSL (retaken June 3)
LEMBERG (retaken June 22)
SECOND
ELEVENTH

CARPATHIANS
THIRD (A.H.)
SECOND (A.H.)
SÜD
Tarnopol

SÜD (G & A.H.)
SEVENTH (A.H.)
Dniester
NINTH

SEVENTH

CZERNOWITZ
Pruth

ROMANIA

General line of the opposing Armies

――――― At end of April
―·―·―·― Mid July
━━━━━ Mid August
·········· Beginning of September
▬ ▬ ▬ End of September
―··― International Frontiers

0            150 km
0        100 miles

N

All countries need their heroes in war and Hindenburg's fame continued to soar. Statues were soon being erected. A museum to him was planned for his home town, Posen. He spent a great deal of his time on what we now call 'public relations', while his staff conducted the affairs of his group of armies. In late October he moved his headquarters to Kovno, on the Niemen River, from where Napoleon had launched his invasion of Russia in 1812. From this base, Hindenburg and Ludendorff contemplated their future operations against Russia, but also began the huge task of organising the conquered Baltic territories. The level of civil government was very low and they planned to introduce thoroughly German values, ahead of actually bringing in German colonists to recreate the old domains of the Teutonic Knights. Ludendorff personally took on a vast amount of administrative work in this wholly unfamiliar sphere of nation building. Despite the victories in the East, they still felt that opportunities had been lost to finish the war there. They pointedly refused to release any of their troops into a reserve for use by General Headquarters and kept up their demand for more men and guns. Their deep hatred of Falkenhayn was absolute and abiding.

1915 had been a remarkable year for Germany and its allies. The Russian armies had been severely punished and driven back into their homeland. A series of Allied attacks had been defeated in the West. The attack on Turkey through the Dardanelles had been checked. The entry of Italy into the war against the Central Powers had been contained. Bulgaria had joined them and, with German and Austrian armies, Mackensen had conquered Serbia, thus opening up secure land communications to Turkey. Germany felt, at last, she was winning the war.

*chapter four*

# The Call to Supreme Command

During the winter of 1915–16 Hindenburg despaired of being able to give the Fatherland the victory it so richly deserved because the Kaiser would not 'stand up' to Falkenhayn and his misguided strategy. He saw the honours bestowed on himself as some sort of compensation for the 'insults and slights' that he had to suffer at the hands of the chief of the Great General Staff. Ludendorff was writing to his friends of his 'bitter hate' towards the man he saw as throwing away opportunities to end the war quickly. In the background Hoffmann wondered if their chances of 'victory' over Falkenhayn were lost forever. This was hardly an edifying spectacle for a nation locked in a life-or-death struggle with a veritable sea of enemies.

Successes in the field ensured that Falkenhayn retained the Kaiser's support; his current opposition to unrestricted submarine warfare (which had nearly brought America into the war against Germany in 1915) secured the support of Chancellor Bethmann-Hollweg. Fully recognising that Germany was engaged in a war of attrition for which she was ill-prepared, Falkenhayn began flirting with those ultra-right organisations in the country that spoke of a German-dominated *Mitteleuropa* controlling the post-war continent. He would rapidly lose the confidence of the chancellor for this overtly political interference. This rift widened as

Falkenhayn seemed to embrace Admiral Tirpitz's renewed and brashly confident calls for all out submarine warfare. Chancellor Bethmann would win this particular round of the battle for the ear of the Kaiser; Tirpitz would be forced to offer his resignation and see it accepted.

German intelligence had deduced that France would have great difficulty in replacing the staggering losses of 1914–15 and the Great General Staff concluded that sustained military pressure on France could force her to the peace table. It was felt that, as British military strength was increasing significantly in 1916, it was time to throw Germany's main effort against the French. Without informing the Imperial Government of his plans, Falkenhayn selected Verdun as an objective that would force the French to fight a defensive battle under a storm of German artillery fire. The intention was to seize the forts on the heights overlooking the town and force the French Army to 'bleed itself white' in their counter-attacks to recover their lost positions.

In February 1916, after an awesome bombardment in which the German artillery delivered two million shells at the rate of 100,000 an hour, the German infantry were told (in an echo of the assurances given to British soldiers on 1 July 1916) that they had only to advance and occupy the shattered trenches of the enemy. Nothing in war is ever that simple. A vicious, unrelenting battle of attrition set in which went on for months. The French steadily fed in more troops, artillery, supplies and equipment to contain every renewed German attack. Losses on both sides were enormous and Crown Prince William, whose Fifth Army bore the brunt of the fighting, was soon calling for the operation to be stood down.

The French showed no signs of coming to the negotiating table and, to add to Falkenhayn's troubles, the Russians showed no signs of having been beaten into submission by their terrible experiences of 1915. Responding once again to a French appeal for increased activity on the Eastern Front to take some of the pressure off the Verdun sector, the Russians attacked the German Tenth Army at Lake Narotch, east of

Vilna. Using a great quantity of artillery and ammunition, but fairly crude infantry tactics, the sheer persistence of the attacks caused some fleeting difficulties but the Germans had observed the preparations and were never overly concerned about the operation. Ludendorff was so confident his local commanders could handle the situation that he was able to leave for Berlin to attend a royal wedding. He, of course, used the opportunity to demand more divisions from the Western Front to develop his own offensive towards Riga. The attrition rates at Verdun made that quite impossible.

The Western Allies had, the previous winter, made an effort to co-ordinate their offensive strategy for the year 1916. The British and French were planning a massive joint attack astride the River Somme (in which French participation had to be drastically reduced because of the Verdun fighting). The Russian contribution was to be an offensive proposed by General Alexei Brusilov against the Austrians on a very wide front. A good deal of careful preparation went into the attack, including the rehearsal over models of enemy entrenchments, the gathering of aerial photographs to identify enemy strong points and batteries, the secret moving up of reserves and the digging of large numbers of 'Russian saps' to get the men across 'no man's land' in safety.

The Austrian front had already been weakened by troops being drawn away for an over-optimistic offensive against the Italians in the Trentino. When the Russians struck early in June, with nothing much in the way of superiority in numbers, but with relatively short and intense artillery preparations, they achieved a stunning series of successes. In a rolling programme of attacks the Russian Eighth, Eleventh and Ninth Armies made large gains of territory, prisoners and captured guns and equipment. Only the Seventh Army failed, precisely because its commander refused to comply with the new style introduced by Brusilov. The Austrians could not work out where the next blow would fall. Within a week they lost nearly 50 per cent of their strength. If the Russian offensive petered out by mid June it was more to do with outrunning their supply lines and the need to reinforce their stretched formations than with enemy resistance.

The Brusilov offensive came as a tremendous shock to the German high command. It triggered a crisis in relations between Germany and Austria-Hungary and led to Falkenhayn making demands on Conrad that ended any pretence of the military independence of the latter. Germany demanded that Austrian troops be transferred from Italy to the Eastern Front; no further Austrian operations were to be undertaken without the approval of German headquarters; as part of a long-term effort to place Germans in tighter control of the whole Eastern Front (something that would never be entirely achieved) the Austrian Seventh Army was obliged to accept a German chief of staff, the excellent Hans von Seeckt.

There was a desperate scrabble to find reserve divisions to prop up the shattered Austrian front. Four came from the West; two were prised out of Hindenburg's command in the north. A counter-attack was launched in mid June east of Kovel. There were no easy victories any more. Progress was dearly paid for and soon ended with the collapse of Austria's Fourth Army. Instead Brusilov renewed his attacks early in July and captured another 30,000 prisoners and thirty guns. The good use of railways to move reserves in a timely fashion saw two German divisions finally halt this phase of the attack as it petered out along the Stokhod River. But Brusilov was able to renew attacks up and down the front well into August and, though his own losses would soar to around the million mark, he had inflicted 1.35 million losses on his enemies (one million Austro-Hungarian; 350,000 German), including the capture of 400,000 prisoners and 500 guns. The vigorous deployment of German reserves and the exhaustion of the attacking armies finally halted this series of offensives but the Austro-German position in the East had been badly dented.

In the West the expected Anglo-French offensive had begun, after a week of artillery preparation, on 1 July 1916. Despite a series of considerable defensive successes north of the Somme on that day, the German Army found itself in the unforgiving grip of an attritional battle that went on for days, weeks and months. The largely British offensive was relentless and implacable and British battle technique improved steadily, especially in the field of infantry–artillery co-operation. The perfection of the 'creeping' barrage by the British artillery was of greater significance than the introduction of the tank onto the Somme battlefield.

Falkenhayn's enemies used these declining fortunes to move against him. Hindenburg wrote directly to the Kaiser saying that Falkenhayn had lost the confidence of the army and implying that he himself was the successor desired by the army. The Kaiser continued to be extremely concerned at the 'Bonapartist' tendencies of his Eastern commanders. Bethmann-Hollweg was now leading a baying pack of critics that included the two Crown Princes, William of Prussia and Rupert of Bavaria, Conrad, and Admiral Tirpitz. The argument was not merely against Falkenhayn but increasingly for Hindenburg to replace him.

In late June 1916 the Kaiser held a conference at Pless to discuss the overall command of the Eastern Front, where the constant fear was that Romania might intervene at any moment, adding a new crisis to an already fraught situation. Forceful demands, orchestrated by Luden-dorff, for Hindenburg to be made commander-in-chief of the whole front were countered by Falkenhayn and Conrad, arguing against the creation of a 'rival supreme command'. Falkenhayn made it clear that he was concerned that the transfer of divisions from East to West would be made 'difficult' by such an arrangement. When the Kaiser heard that political circles in Berlin were demanding Hindenburg's appoint-ment as commander in the East he was doubly incensed and was determined not to be seen to abdicate his role as warlord at the whim of the Berliners. When he was assured that the Austrians would never accept such an arrangement he effectively vetoed the idea. His naval adviser, Admiral Georg von Müller, saw this as a battle won by

Falkenhayn and confided in his diary, 'Let us hope that the German people will not have to pay too dearly for this victory'.

As the British, French and Russian offensives developed in July there were further talks to address the critical situation that was developing. Ludendorff returned from a fruitless meeting in Berlin with Falkenhayn 'in a pretty savage temper' according to Hoffmann. Members of the Kaiser's own cabinet staff were putting pressure on the Austrians to accept Hindenburg as overall commander in the East and seemed to be making some progress in that respect. The Kaiser was not greatly co-operative and continued to insist (somewhat misguidedly) that his generals had, in the last analysis, to obey his orders. Another Russian attack and a spectacular collapse of the Austrians defending Brody led to another Kaiser conference at Pless at the end of July. Bethmann-Hollweg was determined to see an end to the vacillation and was very forceful in his demands. Admiral Müller recorded in his diary on 26 July 1916:

> The Chancellor insists that the appointment of Hindenburg as Supreme Commander East must be carried through and has informed His Majesty that the fate of the Hohenzollern dynasty depends upon it. With Hindenburg he could make a face-saving peace, without him he could do nothing. The Kaiser must not leave Pless before confirming Hindenburg in his new appointment.[1]

The next day the Kaiser went into deep conversation with his army commanders and directed them to resolve their differences. Admiral Müller records that these talks created a very good personal relationship between the Kaiser and Hindenburg, and even towards Ludendorff. Hindenburg was delicate in his choice of words at crucial stages in the discussions. At one stage the 'rather excited' Falkenhayn said, 'Well, if the Herr Field Marshal has the desire and the courage to take the post ...' to which the ever calm and sedate Hindenburg replied, 'The desire, no, but the courage –yes'.[2]

The compromise reached was that Hindenburg, with Ludendorff as his chief of staff, was appointed the commander-in-chief of the Eastern Front for the 500 miles from Riga on the Baltic to the critical area around Brody and Lemberg. This was something like three-quarters of the active front and the Austrian armies below that were under the command of Archduke Charles, with Seeckt as his chief of staff. The Eastern Command moved its headquarters from Kovno in the north to the more central Brest-Litovsk, where they took residence in the old citadel. After some very hot days working from their cramped offices in railway carriages, Ludendorff personally and with great relish organised the complete renovation of the accommodation of the near derelict fortress.

Almost immediately disputes began to arise over the movement of divisions. Falkenhayn understandably resisted demands for troops from the West to be sent to the East, as more and more German divisions were being drawn into the protracted fighting in Picardy. But the request for just one division to be sent from Hindenburg's armies to join Archduke Charles brought on a stiffly worded complaint from the field marshal to his Kaiser. This received an equally stiff rebuke from the supreme warlord. Ludendorff made the point that a very high proportion of the German forces in the East were Landwehr or Landsturm units. There were 'too many men of the oldest classes on the Eastern Front, and we did not like to place such men in the hottest corners'. As it happened the only reserve available in the whole of Hindenburg's command was one brigade of cavalry and some artillery and machine-gun units. The Russians ended all offensive operations in the north and central sectors and concentrated their efforts against the sagging Austro-Hungarian armies in the south. Ludendorff was able to make extensive tours of the Austro-Hungarian formations and made detailed recommendations for the improvement of their training for modern warfare.

Ludendorff and Hoffmann tried to persuade the field marshal to threaten to resign if Falkenhayn was not replaced as chief of the Great General Staff. The old Prussian loyalty to the Kaiser would not permit

him to take such a step. These two then threatened their own resigna-
tions if Hindenburg would not take a firmer stand on their many griev-
ances. A request for an audience with the Kaiser was refused and the
subsequent letter of complaint sent under Hindenburg's signature to
Chancellor Bethmann-Hollweg triggered the final crisis. He had also
received letters criticising Falkenhayn's grip on the overall war situation from within the Great General Staff itself, penned by the brilliant
Colonel Max Bauer. Against a background of repeated letters of
complaint and threats of resignation by the Eastern army command,
Bethmann-Hollweg put pressure on the Kaiser to end the fratricide by
dismissing Falkenhayn. The Kaiser stubbornly refused to bow to outside
pressure in what he regarded as his last great prerogative, the command
of 'his' army. It was then Falkenhayn's great misfortune to assure the
Kaiser that Romania would remain neutral until after the September
harvest just a few days before she declared war on Austria-Hungary. As
600,000 new troops entered the fray against Germany and her allies the
Kaiser invited Hindenburg and his chief of staff to Pless to seek their
advice on this latest turn of events. Falkenhayn went to the Kaiser and
insisted that he had only one military adviser and that was the chief of
the Great General Staff. If the Kaiser received Hindenburg for that
purpose then Falkenhayn said that he would resign. The Kaiser replied,
'As you wish', the deed was done and Falkenhayn 'left unobtrusively
for Berlin'. Thus it was that on the date considered to be the anniversary
of the victory at Tannenberg, 29 August, Field Marshal Paul von
Hindenburg was appointed Chief of Staff of the Armies in the Field
of the German Empire.

Ludendorff was promoted to infantry general and was invited to
become the second chief of staff, a wholly new post. He deferred, saying
that there can be only one 'chief' and selected for himself the title First
Quartermaster General. It was implied that he would share fully in the
responsibility for all decisions and measures taken to bring the war to
a successful conclusion. He noted in his memoirs that he and his revered

chief never again returned to the Eastern Front. (Field Marshal Prince Leopold of Bavaria became the new commander-in-chief in the East, with Colonel Hoffmann as his chief of staff.) Ludendorff wrote, 'My position was a thankless one ... a sacred desire to do and think of nothing that did not contribute to bring the war to a victorious end ... The task was perfectly enormous. The awful feeling of responsibility did not leave me for a single instant'.[3]

On 31 August 1916 a great conference was held between the new high command and representatives of the government and the Kaiser's cabinet to review the war situation. The navy began lobbying immediately for a resumption of unrestricted submarine warfare. Whilst they were anxious not to let the navy remain 'idle', Hindenburg asked for the matter to be put on hold until after the Romanians had been dealt with and Ludendorff suggested that Germany did not need to do anything to add to its tally of enemies at that time. Italy had just declared war on Germany, just as Germany declared against Romania; Holland and Denmark could both be pushed into the arms of the Western Allies by the war at sea; America's intervention was always on the horizon.

The General Staff had, while still under Falkenhayn's leadership, already taken steps to deal with the almost inevitable Romanian declaration of war. German, Austrian, Bulgarian and Turkish troops had been assembled close to her borders; Mackensen was in theatre as a commander; Falkenhayn himself would join him before too long as an army commander. Before they had visited the Western Front or made a serious study of its requirements Ludendorff ordered the complete cessation of the Verdun offensive (for which he had the support of the Crown Prince) and sent some divisions out of France for use against Romania. It was fortunate for the new high command to be in place to oversee the decisive defeat of Romania and add to their lustre as the bringers of victory for the German people. It goes without saying that a new wave of euphoria swept over Germany as the 'national hero' and his trusty assistant were elevated to the supreme command.

*chapter five*

# Seeing the Whole Picture

The Army High Command (*Oberste Heeresleitung* – OHL) remained at Pless in Upper Silesia, where it was conveniently close to Austrian head-quarters at Teschen. A new chief of operations was appointed, the industrious if stubborn and quarrelsome Lieutenant Colonel Georg Wetzell, significantly a veteran of the Western Front. The brilliant intriguer Lieutenant Colonel Max Bauer continued as chief of Section Two, responsible for making the army's needs known to industry, and Nicolai remained at Intelligence (Section IIIb, which took on a greater role in economic and political analysis and devising propaganda for both military and civilian consumption). Ludendorff only brought one officer with him from *OberOst* – Major von Vollard-Bockelberg as chief of administration. He was content to let the excellent Hoffmann remain in the East, effectively commanding the whole front as the chief of staff to the amiable and compliant Prince Leopold of Bavaria.

On 5 September 1916 Hindenburg and Ludendorff left by special train to visit the commanders on the Western Front, with news of the first successes against Romania in the Dobruja speeding them on their way. Ludendorff was able to travel with his wife, Margarethe, between Frankfurt and Metz. She leaves a vivid picture of the triumphal procession of their train through Germany.

On 7 September William, Crown Prince of Prussia met Hindenburg and Ludendorff on Monmedy station – the crack company of von
Rohr's storm battalion forming a guard of honour. Ludendorff was
particularly impressed by this unit, wearing the new steel helmet and
so renowned for its innovative tactics that it was used as a demonstration
unit in the training programmes of the Western armies. A discussion
of the situation on the Crown Prince's front took place on the journey
to Charleville, and on 8 September the army group commanders, the
commanders of the Fourth, First and Second Armies, and all the chiefs
of staff were summoned to a conference at the Crown Prince Rupert
of Bavaria's headquarters at Cambrai. Hindenburg carried out important ceremonial duties during this trip – awarding the Crown Prince of
Bavaria and the Duke of Württemburg their field marshal's batons.
Ludendorff was quite alarmed at the open desire of Prince Rupert for
an immediate peace, a 'peace of understanding' without annexations
and other such demands.

This conference was an important learning experience for the two
commanders who had so frequently demanded reinforcement from the
Western Front. It is to their joint credit that they so quickly saw that
they had been unduly critical of their predecessor and the way scarce
resources had to be balanced and conserved across the entire continent
and its several battlefields. Hindenburg later wrote: 'I will not hesitate
to admit that it was only now that I fully realised all that the Western
armies had done hitherto'. Ludendorff repeated his first refrain on
assuming high command: 'I began to realise what a task the field marshal
and I had undertaken in our new spheres'.

In a one-day conference they heard detailed reports from the men
tasked with withstanding the powerful Anglo-French offensive astride
the Somme in Picardy. It was a tale of shortages – of artillery and shells,
of aircraft, of fresh divisions, and the impossibility of giving the fighting
formations proper periods to rest and refit. Ludendorff absorbed the
information avidly and fired back a number of searching questions that

provided him with more food for thought. He quickly decided that the manner in which the defensive was being conducted was adding greatly to the material and manpower losses being sustained. He confirmed his suspicion that the deep dugouts of permanent positions had a deleterious effect on the fighting prowess of the troops. He actually referred to the defence as 'flabby'. He favoured a looser type of defence that allowed the infantryman more flexibility in his response to attacks. 'In the end of ends, infantry is the deciding factor in every battle. I was in the infantry myself and was body and soul an infantryman'.[1] It was their discipline and patriotism that helped the ordinary soldier through a burdensome life in the trenches. Trench fighting degraded the offensive spirit of the troops and led them to rely far too much on hand grenades as a personal weapon, to the detriment of their rifle skills: 'The infantry soldier had forgotten his shooting through the use of grenades. He had to relearn it. He had to acquire confidence in his weapon, and that meant he had to become the master of it. That was easier to advise than to accomplish'.[2] It is not surprising that exactly these same lessons of the Somme fighting were being learnt by British staff officers at every level and these sentiments would find their way into their training manuals issued soon after it.

Ludendorff was soon at work organising better battlefield communications, improved infantry–artillery co-operation (which would soon see German divisional commanders having a much greater control of artillery assets allotted to them), insisting that the German Air Force spend less time skirmishing in the air and more time spotting for the guns, and setting staff officers to work on new defensive tactics. He saw the need for more long-range guns, for a light machine gun and the organisation of special 'sharpshooting' machine-gun companies, and for more trench mortars and grenade throwers. He also remembered Rohr's storm troopers and began to think how their fighting methods might be used more widely. But the initial task was to defend the Western Front at least until the end of 1916, when victory over Romania might

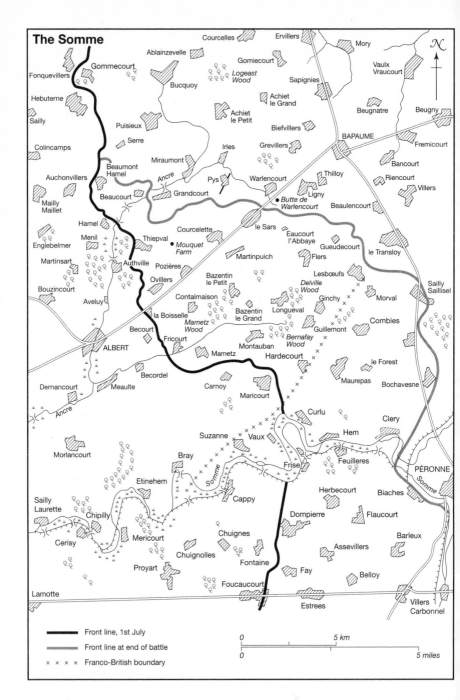

# The Somme

Courcelles
Ervillers
Mory
Vaulx
Vraucourt
Ablainzevelle
Gommiecourt
Gommecourt
Fonquevillers
Sapignies
Beugny
Bucquoy
Beugnatre
Hebuterne
*Logeast
Wood*
Achiet
le Grand
Sailly
Puisieux
Achiet
le Petit
Biefvillers
BAPAUME
Fremicourt
Colincamps
Serre
Irles
Grevillers
Bancourt
Miraumont
Riencourt
Beaumont
Hamel
Warlencourt
Thilloy
Villers
Ancre
Pys
Ligny
Beaucourt
Grandcourt
• *Butte de
Warlencourt*
Beaulencourt
le Transloy
Sailly
Saillisel
Hamel
Courcelette
le Sars
Menil
Thiepval
Eaucourt
l'Abbaye
Gueudecourt
Englebelmer
• *Mouquet
Farm*
Martinpuich
Flers
Martinsart
Authville
Pozières
Lesbœufs
*Delville
Wood*
Ginchy
Morval
Bouzincourt
Ovillers
Bazentin
le Petit
Aveluy
Contalmaison
Bazentin
le Grand
Longueval
Guillemont
Combles
la Boiselle
*Mametz
Wood*
Becourt
Fricourt
Montauban
*Bernafay
Wood*
le Forest
ALBERT
Mametz
Hardecourt
Maurepas
Bochavesne
Becordel
Dernancourt
Meaulte
Carnoy
Maricourt
Curlu
Clery
*Ancre*
Suzanne
Vaux
Hem
Morlancourt
Bray
Frise
Feuilleres
PÉRONNE
Etinehem
*Somme*
Cappy
Herbecourt
Biaches
*Somme*
Sailly
Laurette
Chipilly
Dompierre
Flaucourt
Cerisy
Mericourt
Chuignes
Fontaine
Asservillers
Barleux
Chuignolles
Belloy
Proyart
Fay
Foucaucourt
Lamotte
Estrees
Villers
Carbonnel

| | Front line, 1st July |
|---|---|
| | Front line at end of battle |
| × × × × | Franco-British boundary |

0                    5 km
0                    5 miles

give the Empire and its resources something of a breathing space. Part of this overall strategy was the immediate start of work on a massive new defensive system called the Siegfried Line (popularly called the Hindenburg Line) built across the arc of the great central salient on the Western Front, to which the German Army would fall back at the right moment and, by reducing its front, release many divisions for a much-needed reserve.

The Crown Prince William recalled how Hindenburg summed up the strategic situation at the close of the Cambrai conference:

> The amount of such assistance to be given was only to be limited by the necessity of holding our present line everywhere, especially at Verdun, where the French, despite the fighting on the Somme, still had strong forces concentrated.
>
> We were also informed from the same authoritative source that the Eastern front, as far as could humanly be foreseen, was firmly established from Kovel to Riga, but on the Carpathian front and in Volhynia and Galicia the further support of German troops would be necessary. In view of the poor quality of the Austrian troops, their intermixture with German forces, even down to the smallest units, was of the utmost value; nevertheless, our strategic prospects were limited by the possibilty of a repulse in this area. The situation on the Italian, Caucasian and Macedonian fronts was likely, as the Field Marshal considered, to remain unchanged at the moment. He pointed out that despite the strain on our resources both in the East and in the West, we must still aim at definite results during the present year, and, as things stood at the present, these could only be secured against Romania, whose army appeared at first sight to be of inferior quality. For this purpose and in addition to those forces required for the above tasks, yet further dispatches of troops would be necessary, and these would be reinforced by new formations.

'We must hope', the Field Marshal concluded, 'to hold our ground till the end of 1916 and finish up with a decisive victory.'

The subsequent regulation of the necessary details involved, as far as my Army was concerned, serious demands on the energies of the front-line troops and the organising ability of the staffs; but we all came away from this memorable conference with the feeling that the Army and the country could look with confidence to the new High Command.[3]

After the grim experience of the Somme, Verdun and Galician fighting the German Army was undergoing a blizzard of change. Its infantry divisions visibly shrank in size, in part because reinforcements went to create new divisions, in part because of the dearth of experienced officers. Ludendorff noted that an officer in the 'Old Army' used to serve fifteen years before he got command of a company. Now companies went to young men of two or three years' service, and he doubted their ability to handle more than 200 men at a time. He would later regret the reluctance of the German Army to promote veteran non-commissioned officers to officer rank.[4] Firepower was added to the divisions to compensate for reductions in personnel and an increased level of control over artillery assets assigned to the division in battle.

As Germany braced itself for a series of renewed offensives by the Entente powers, her military posture became even more defence minded. Cavalry divisions were dismounted, and reserve cavalry formations (Landwehr and Landsturm) were completely disbanded. Their horses were desperately needed by the artillery and supply services. Greater reliance was placed on permanent fortified positions. 'The construction of positions in the West was systematically revised, from the point of view of the new theory of distribution in depth and the most careful adaptation to the ground.'[5] Besides the two new strategic lines (the Siegfried Line and the Drocourt-Queant Switch), the positions in the Flanders, Arras, Verdun and Alsace-Lorraine sectors were all strengthened in accordance with the new principles. Ludendorff fretted on the burden that all this extra labour placed on the infantry when they should have been resting and training. He mused that the armies in the field didn't seem to mind the work so much when it was deep defences they were constructing; he and his staff would have much preferred the time to be spent absorbing and practising the new defence doctrines.

These doctrines had been a long time gestating and were based on the experiences of the German Army dating back to the huge French offensives in the Champagne in 1915. There a Colonel Fritz von Lossberg had observed how German defences placed on the reverse slopes of ridges under attack had avoided enemy artillery fire and had been able to break up the leading waves of attacking infantry, and render them vulnerable to counter-attack. This was worked up into a theory advocating a deep but loosely held 'forward zone' that functioned to absorb and disorganise the attackers, and a 'main line of resistance' that functioned partly as protection to the field artillery and partly as the base from which the counter-attacks would be launched. The new theory gave the front-line infantryman a great deal of initiative and countenanced his retreating in any direction he chose to avoid the worst of the enemy attack, before making rapid counter-attacks to regain the lost ground. If the opportunity for a quick riposte passed, then more seriously organised counter-attacks, often involving specially prepared *Gegenangriff* divisions, were to be made as soon as possible. This new level of flexibility in defence was highly controversial and many of the old school, wedded to the notion of 'not giving an inch', objected to it. Colonel Bauer and Captain Geyer of the Great General Staff wrote up a manual on 'The Defensive Battle' to get the debate going. Even within the ranks of the staff there was great misgiving. Ludendorff wrote, 'The controversy raged furiously in my Staff; I myself had to intervene to advocate the new tactics'.[6] Just as in the British Expeditionary Force at the same time, German higher formations were also encapsulating their battle experience and General Fritz von Below's army headquarters produced an excellent 'Manual for the Training of Infantry in War' which won over many other combatants and greatly assisted the adoption of the new ideas. The Great General Staff began producing manuals for all the specialist arms to back up the new doctrine, including pamphlets on how to fight in the new defensive positions that were organised in such depth. From this vigorous intellectual debate there came a major programme of training for the whole army. Special courses were run at a school at Valenciennes for senior and General Staff officers to master the new doctrine; the Crown Prince William ran a separate school for his army group at Sedan. Large new responsibilities were placed on the regimental officers to retrain their troops, and the divisional commander was charged with seeing that his formation was thoroughly familiar with the new expectations. Commanders were still there to lead and instruct their troops; the General Staff was still there to help and advise him in that task. Ludendorff took a great personal interest in the selection of officers for service on the General Staff, and brought in numbers of regimental officers with practical war experience.[7] It was always his ideal that he would be able to teach these new doctrines to the armies of Germany's allies, but in reality this had to remain very much a dream.

By mid-September Hindenburg and Ludendorff were back at OHL Pless and beginning the enormous task of reorganising the whole military effort of Germany and her allies to bring the war to a successful conclusion as soon as possible. A routine of unremitting hard work established itself. Ludendorff was at his desk by 8 a.m. Hindenburg would visit him for a survey of the overnight reports from the various fighting fronts. Hindenburg explained that these meetings could be quite brief: 'We knew each other's thoughts. The decisions were, therefore, usually a matter of a few sentences; indeed, very often a few words were all that were required to establish that mutual understanding which served the General as a basis for his further working-out of the plans'. For the rest of the morning Hindenburg would be involved in seeing important visitors, Allied generals, journalists or the representatives of neutral countries. Much is made of his leisurely walks while engaged in these activities but it was an important part of the duties of a commander-in-chief. The briefest glimpse of the diaries of Sir Douglas Haig will show that his time was equally in demand from a constant stream of visitors and that he, too, had to make time for regular exercise to keep him fit for the burdens of high command (in his case, plenty of horse riding). Every day at noon Hindenburg and Ludendorff together made a report to the Kaiser of the military situation; the discussions would often involve members of the Kaiser's personal cabinets and/or government ministers. After a simple lunch Ludendorff would return to his staff duties and Hindenburg would spend most of the afternoon answering the avalanche of letters that descended on him daily. Dinner at 8 p.m. was usually with some important personages, whom Hindenburg would entertain while Ludendorff returned to his desk at about 9.30 p.m. to work until midnight, or even later. The official artist, Vogel, was back in residence and struggled to keep up with the demand for paintings and sketches of the national heroes.

Their visitors would regularly include the Kaiser, the King of Bulgaria, the Austrian commander, Conrad von Hötzendorf, the Turkish commander Enver Pasha and the grand vizier Talaat Pasha, Count Tisza of Hungary and German political figures. They were especially courted by German industrialists, scientists, shipping magnates and bankers who saw them as the new tribunes of their drive for victory, annexations and reparations. At last they had found a team of commanders equally dedicated to ultimate victory as themselves. Newspaper men, especially the still neutral Americans, were well received, as were awestruck trade union leaders whom the high command were keen to flatter with their attention.

At OHL, under the benign overall leadership of Hindenburg, everyone worked with a renewed sense of purpose as Ludendorff gradually harnessed the enormous talent residing there and gave it a new sense of direction. General Wilhelm Groener, who had served under Falkenhayn and his chief of staff, Tappen, made this interesting observation in October 1916:

> One can work extremely well with Ludendorff. The new command is entirely different from the previous one with the Tappen shortsightedeness ... Hindenburg is extraordinarily versed in military history and has an unusually clear mind. He is also gifted with a very well aimed and appropriate wit and sense of humour. Falkenhayn and Tappen always made him out to be a sort of fool, purely a front man for Ludendorff. That is not the case. I have also changed my opinion of Ludendorff, which was clouded by the atmosphere of the OHL.[8]

Crown Prince William had, at the time of Tannenberg, hailed Hindenburg as 'the teacher of the German General Staff' and it must be recognised that Hindenburg's pre-war reputation as an expert in strategy and tactics was considerable and well founded.

If the Cambrai conference opened the eyes of the new commanders to the huge task facing the German armies in the West, presenting them with new demands for more and better arms and munitions, they had now to face the total problem of mobilising the whole economy and nation for the life-and-death struggle into which they were locked. Like all other combatants Germany had entered the war in 1914 expecting it to be of great violence but of relatively short duration. To the problems of deadlock on the Western Front and the vast spaces and seemingly endless Russian manpower in the East was now added the allied naval blockade. In no time at all German shipping was swept from the seas and her booming pre-war exports and imports were suddenly reduced to what could be carried through the neutral ports of Holland, Denmark and Scandinavia. Shortages and rationing were not far behind.

As early as 28 January 1915 the government took over the control of the entire grain production in a quasi-public Grain Corporation and it set a bread ration at half a pound per day (a 50 per cent reduction in the average pre-war consumption). As grain was not available to feed livestock there was an extraordinary slaughter of pigs from February to May 1915. Germany gorged itself on pork products for some time and then the shortages began to escalate. At first things were just difficult to obtain – milk, butter, cooking oil, and all overseas produce (coffee, fruit etc.) By the end of 1915 things were more serious, with the introduction of official 'meatless' days and 'fatless' days to eke out shrinking reserves. The Royal Navy had hermetically sealed Germany from the outside world.

As casualties rose and hardship increased at home, the National Foundation for War Widows found itself helping four million families (eleven million people) who were living in real poverty as a result of the war. During one of their fundraising drives in August 1915, this organisation erected a thirty-two foot high, 28-ton wooden statue of Field Marshal Hindenburg in Berlin and invited people to purchase nails to hammer into it. Before long the 'wooden titan' was turned into a gleaming monument with 90,000 iron and 10,000 silver nails. The idea was copied all across Germany; the Hindenburg cult was well established in the cause of war charities.

In 1915 the German people still expected victory soon. Their soldiers defended their conquests in the West, won massive victories in the East, and conquered the Serbs. They were not told of the desperate condition of their principal ally, Austria-Hungary, but they saw the Turks defeat the entente efforts in the Dardanelles and the Central Powers were joined by Bulgaria. There was still a degree of enthusiasm for the war effort and shortages just had to be tolerated for the duration. War loans were subscribed; drives to recover badly needed metals of all types (pots and pans, kettles, brass door knobs and knockers, bells etc.) were still productive. The year 1916 was a more severe trial. The scale of the fighting in the West reached truly appalling levels, the Russians seemed far from beaten in the East, and the Italians and the

Romanians joined the list of Germany's enemies. Now meat was in very short supply at home; bread become more and more adulterated with both vegetable and mineral additives; beer production was half its pre-war level. The bread ration had to be cut to seven ounces a day, and meat, potatoes, sugar and cooking oils and fats were all tightly rationed. The increasing number of disgusting ersatz products did little to improve the dreary life of the German civilian. Most damaging to morale was the fact that there was plenty of food available for sale in the countryside, if you could afford it. Every weekend saw a mass flight from the towns to the country where a blatant and thriving black market operated under the noses of the military and civil authorities. With most leather and cloth production going to the armed forces for uniforms, boots and accoutrements, there was a total lack of these items for civilian use. Bizarre creations of paper and vegetable by-products had to be worn as clothing; wood was the principal component of new shoes. Add the almost total absence of anything that could decently be called soap and the normally fastidious German civilian began to ask when and if the war would ever be over. Unsurprisingly the summer of 1916 saw the first strikes by German workers in Berlin and other cities where the demand for 'bread' (better wages) was combined with calls for peace.

Then came the catastrophe of the winter of 1916–17. The potato harvest largely failed. Of the expected fifty-five million tons, only twenty-five million were gathered in. Famine became a very real threat to the German people. In desperation they were obliged to eat large quantities of a fairly unpalatable variety of turnip. This 'turnip winter', as it is indelibly imprinted on the German civilian consciousness, was a terrible blow to home morale. It coincided with a major crisis in coal production where so much was taken up by heavy industry and the railways that there had to be huge cuts in the amounts available for domestic fuel. In a freezing cold winter, which was bad enough, there was the added misery of frozen and burst water pipes and a general deterioration of the housing stock. This increase in universal misery helps to explain the rash of articles in the press highlighting the new problem of youth delinquency. The combination of the absence of fathers away at the wars and the wretchedness of life on rations, together with the opposite allure of too much money in their pockets as a consequence of plenty of 'reserved' war work at relatively high wages, made German commentators think that an entire generation of youths had become utterly ungovernable.

Against this increasingly serious social background the German High Command had to intervene to mobilise the nation and the economy for total war. Ludendorff had studied the dire condition of the economy and had noted the role of the naval blockade in exacerbating the problem: 'In this death grapple Germany and her Allies had been cut off from the world by a monstrous conspiracy and thrown back upon their own resources'.[9] Back in 1890 Moltke had opined that the next great European war might last for seven years, or it could last for thirty. Ludendorff was quite bitter that between them the civilian government and Falkenhayn's OHL had failed to organise the nation state for such a struggle:

> In the situation in which the Field Marshal and I found ourselves, and in view of our whole conception of the character of this war and the enemy's determination to destroy us, we considered it essential to develop the economic, physical and moral strength of the Fatherland to the highest degree. GHQ's demands on the Imperial Government comprised man-power, war material and moral resolution.[10]

As early as 31 August 1916 Hindenburg had contacted the War Ministry to insist on a dramatic increase in war production, making the interesting point that on the battlefield the power of machinery must replace the muscle power of men and horses. With an appeal akin to that of the French Revolution's 'La patrie en danger!' he called for the home front to mobilise returned wounded men, prisoners of war, women and youths for war production. He offered to release several thousand skilled workers from the army to boost production, and could not know then that industry would claim many tens of thousands of such men. Sunday working was to be introduced; non-essential industries that had not died for lack of materials would be shut down forthwith.

OHL began to produce a series of production targets to fulfil what it thought to be necessary to bring the war to a successful conclusion. Based on August 1916 production figures, they demanded that gunpowder production be doubled to 12,000 tons per month; artillery doubled to 3,000 pieces per month; and machine guns tripled to 7,000 per month. A thousand new aircraft and a thousand new aircraft engines per month would also be required. Ludendorff's memoirs recall that all the extra requirements of industrialised warfare had to be allowed for – poison gases, gas shells, smoke shells, motor transport, light machine guns, and armour-piercing bullets. The last named item shows that German military leaders were conscious of the arrival on the battlefield of armoured fighting vehicles ('tanks') in the armies of Great Britain and France. Ludendorff made the deliberate decision not to go in for the development and production of German tanks for the simple reason that German industry was stretched to the absolute limit producing what was needed already.

In the fervour created by the recent change in leadership, this mobilisation was inevitably called the 'Hindenburg programme'. Ludendorff was characteristically generous in sharing the credit:

> The whole programme was a complicated mental achievement, intended as it was to meet future requirements rather than present necessities. Most of the credit is due to Colonel Bauer, of my staff. It was only definitely settled after several conferences on Berlin, and received the name of the Hindenburg programme, although the programme put forward by GHQ was not confined to the proposals for increased munitions production, but involved demands for more men and moral support.[11]

It is certainly true that Ludendorff carefully supervised all this aspect of staff work and added enormously to his personal workload. In fact Bauer would later say that: 'too much rests on Ludendorff: all domestic and foreign policy, economic questions, the matter of food supply, etc. He is greatly overtaxed, usually totally exhausted, also often-times nervous'.

The heads of heavy and chemical industry and their financiers were hugely enthusiastic about this new and forceful directive, if only because they could see their revenues and profits mounting astronomically. We should never forget that this war was fought by rival capitalist economies and there were huge fortunes being made on every side as a result of it. When the industry chiefs asked Colonel Bauer for how long these new production targets might be expected to be in place, he thought the middle of June 1917 should see the war brought to a successful conclusion.

OHL used the new sense of direction to tighten its grip on the War Ministry. On 1 October 1916 it set up a Weapons and Munitions Procurement Agency to replace the old Ordnance Master's Office and by 1 November had installed General Groener as head of a new *Kriegsamt* (War Office) which had 'direction of all matters pertaining to the recruitment, deployment and feeding of workers as well as the procurement of raw materials, weapons and munitions for the overall war effort'. It assumed special responsibility for the vital coal, iron and steel industries.

Next it turned to the question of manpower and its proper mobilisation. Since 31 July 1914 Article 68 of the Reich Constitution had been in force – the Law of the State of Siege. (This harsh measure was based on the old Prussian law of 1851 designed to prevent a repetition of the 1848 revolutions.) Under it the general officers commanding the twenty-four army corps districts and the permanent fortress commanders acquired considerable powers of arbitrary arrest to control dissent, the press, postal censorship, food supply and workers' activities. They could even suspend articles of the constitution relating to civil liberties as they saw fit. Chancellor Bethmann-Hollweg wondered aloud how this equated with the *Burgfriede* (social truce) declared by the Kaiser on the first day of the war, when he publicly stated that he no longer recognised social classes, only Germans! Legal chaos ensued as some generals lashed out at any criticism of the armed forces and others were more aware of the importance of not antagonising the working population whose support was so obviously vital to the war effort. These military governors found themselves increasingly embroiled in social and economic affairs such as the drive for more manpower, both military and industrial. Soldiers found themselves mired in the minutiae of directing labour from one sector of the economy to the other, and in the control of a relentlessly spreading dissent. It did not help that technically they were not answerable to OHL and some maintained a sturdy independence for their district, especially in the kingdoms and principalities that made up the German Reich. They could, of course, be expected to follow the spirit of OHL directives, and certainly Section IIIb's ideas on press censorship were closely observed.

Responding to the complaints of heavy industry that their work was hampered by the inadequate regulation of the supply of labour, Hindenburg began to put pressure on the chancellor for an improved mobilisation of the German people for military and industrial service. He wanted exemptions from army service reduced and the upper age limit for the 'active' army raised to 50. He also wanted to restrict worker movement within industry and proposed a new Labour Office to control wages. Bethmann-Hollweg and the War Minister Wild von Hohenborn both resisted these demands, partly because they resented OHL interference in government matters, and partly because they believed that a free market in labour preserved social cohesion and allowed the high wages offered by the major war industries to ensure that they would never be short of workers. It was the great industrial leaders who then led a campaign to denounce the war minister as lacking the necessary resolve.

SEEING THE WHOLE PICTURE

When OHL proposed the idea of the *Kriegsamt* under the capable General Groener to take control of the war economy, the chancellor accepted the idea only if it was made a part of the War Ministry. Ludendorff was then able to appear conciliatory when he agreed to this, provided that Hohenborn was asked to resign. The Military Cabinet ordered Hohenborn to go on 28 October 1916, and the compliant General Stein replaced him. The German High Command had got its first taste of forcing the resignation of a government minister – an unfortunate precedent.

Hindenburg then stepped up the pressure for further control of the labour market. He wanted the conscription of all males between the ages of 15 and 60 and their enforced allocation to the military or industry as necessary. He suggested that all universities, in Germany and all the occupied countries, should be closed down to prevent women from colonising them in the absence of male students. He also fiercely resisted any demands for pay parity from women workers. They were, of course, flocking into industrial employment but at about half the pay rates for men. This extraordinary reluctance to properly mobilise women for Germany's war effort was to repeat itself in the next world war. Despite the reductions in rations the Hindenburg programme still expected increased working hours in industry.

Finally OHL presented an Auxiliary Service Law calling for the conscription of all males between 15 and 60. Bethmann-Hollweg opposed it; the workers were deeply suspicious of it and prevented their trades union leaders from accepting it too readily. Groener preferred to work with labour organisations than to dominate them and he cleverly engaged in discussions of 'war socialism' for the good of the Fatherland. OHL mounted a ferocious press campaign against the chancellor, releasing letters that suggested that the war would have to end soon without this new law. All the economic ills of the nation – inflation, profiteering, shortages, unrest and 'excessively high' wages – were blamed on those resisting the patriotic demands of OHL. It was on

2 December 1916 that the Reichstag, by 235 votes to 14, passed the Auxiliary Service Law, calling for all males between 17 (a concession demanded to maintain the fiction of the Reichstag's independence) and 60 not already engaged in war work to become available for 'patriotic duty' under the direction of the *Kriegsamt*. The law was hopelessly vague, imposing tight restrictions on the working class but leaving the middle class free to describe their employment as 'necessary' or otherwise pretty much as they saw fit. It restricted the movement of workers between jobs and allowed for fines for those refusing to take up assigned work. But in the last analysis it could not prevent the very capitalist employers who had been calling for it, from enticing workers away from rival firms with higher wage offers, so that they could secure contracts and profits for themselves.

It was indicative of Germany's structural political weakness that the high command had to devise the Hindenburg programme and take upon itself the task that should have been carried out by a proper government. While one might admire the energy and clear-headed foresight of the generals who grasped this nettle, it has to be said that there were aspects of it that owed more to propaganda for home consumption. The War Ministry had already put into effect a series of manufacturing targets that raised gunpowder production to 8,000 tons a month by December 1915 and 10,000 tons a month by July 1916; artillery production was reaching 2,000 pieces per month. The clarion demands of the Hindenburg programme were already well on the way to being achieved. Ludendorff was actually able to switch factories away from artillery production to the more urgent task of building locomotives. The production of rifles was grossly in excess of the army's requirements. Similarly the 'Hindenburg' demand for a 'tripling' of machine-gun output to 7,000 a month was well on the way to achievement, with production hitting 7,200 per month by July 1917 and continuing to soar by the autumn to the utterly unusable total of 14,400 guns per month. One part of the economy turned out weaponry that stood idle in warehouses, while other sectors failed to keep up with the heavy demands made upon them. Total steel production in 1917 actually declined and the rail transportation system, on which so much else of the economy and war-making depended, went into serious crisis for want of locomotives, rolling stock, workers and coal.

In a similar way the Auxiliary Service Law promised much more than it actually delivered. Groener had said he could direct 200,000 workers from the civil economy to military agencies. By April 1917 barely 60,000 had reported for duty; the most it ever reached was 118,000 by June, of whom 75,000 were women and 4,000 old men and boys. Instead the army had to release over a million men from the military to vital war work, especially on the railways. This was to have a serious effect on the front-line strength of German units. Ludendorff himself was soon denouncing the law as 'neither fish nor fowl ... but a shadow of the reality we desired'. The industrial chiefs were aghast as workers used every avenue opened to them by the new law, which included workers' councils to mediate between workers and management, to improve their conditions. Where some 10 per cent of workers had changed jobs before August 1916, the ratio shot up to 40 per cent in 1917, which proved to be positively harmful to the war economy.

Towards the end of 1916 the chancellor, who had been inviting American President Woodrow Wilson to get involved as a possible peace mediator since September, made a speech in the Reichstag expressing Germany's desire for an end to the war by negotiation. In public Hindenburg and Ludendorff reacted so angrily that they were able to force the resignation of the Foreign Minister, Jagow, and see him replaced by Arthur Zimmermann. But at dinner with Admiral Müller, Ludendorff had shown himself to be 'extraordinarily clear-headed and sure of his goal'. In his memoirs Ludendorff stated quite clearly that he encouraged the chancellor in his 'peace initiative', carefully timed to become public just after the fall of Bucharest and at the flood tide of German military success in the East. His claim to be genuinely ready for a peace of justice and reconciliation (which would have included demands for annexations and reparations) has to be tempered by his certain knowledge that President Wilson's proposals were so woolly that they would be angrily spurned by the Entente powers, 'such as to leave no doubt of their intention to annihilate us'. It has to be remembered that Ludendorff, and all the German military leaders, fought in the certain knowledge that their country had been reluctantly forced into a war not of their choosing, by powers that sought their destruction as a great nation. All this was co-ordinated by the vengeful and malevolent 'England', and Ludendorff found himself admiring the iron determination of its leader, David Lloyd George, and the skill with which England constantly succeeded in showing Germany in the worst possible light on the world stage.

Germany was about to hand their enemy the greatest of all propaganda coups. The question of the correct use of the German submarine fleet was again being discussed. After the brief period of unrestricted use in 1915, which had turned all neutral countries against them, the Germans had reverted to obeying certain rules of engagement that required them to force the surrender of merchant ships and the evacuation of their crews and passengers before sending them to the bottom. Hindenburg was on record as approving of the unrestricted use of submarines as a weapon of war against any and all shipping visiting enemy ports, but only at a time of convenience to the army as part of a larger war plan. The prospect of European neutral countries declaring war on Germany was an immediate problem that had to be taken into account. Holland alone could field 500,000 new troops and would pose the greatest possible threat to the German armies on the Western Front. The borders of both Denmark and Holland would have to be guarded and the troops were not available for that task until after Romania was defeated. The threat of the entry into the war of the United States of America was obviously the biggest concern for the German government and armed forces. Ludendorff thought that

American industry was so completely geared up for production on behalf of the Western Allies, that the actual intervention of her armed forces would be almost marginal. It would be at least a year before American armies arrived in France in large enough numbers to make a decisive impact. The German Army and Navy would have to force a result before that happened.

A mounting tide of pressure had been building since the appointment of Hindenburg and Ludendorff to supreme command. It emanated from the navy and from industrialists, shipping magnates and right-wing politicians. Typical is this letter of 19 September 1916 from Arnd von Holtzendorf, director of the Hamburg-Amerika shipping line, to Admiral Müller:

> For a year now I have followed the principle which Hindenburg has recently adopted for his slogan: 'First weigh the cost and then dare', and I have weighed things up for so long that there are no longer any grounds for wavering or for half-measures. Let us attack England now and destroy her shipping with all the means in our power or else we shall bleed to death and we shall have deserved our collapse...[12]

Bethmann-Hollweg countered with arguments about adding to Germany's list of enemies, and his point about Holland's half a million troops certainly curbed the army's sudden enthusiasm for an unrestricted war at sea. But his various offers of a partial submarine offensive – singling out all shipping using certain North African ports, or permitting the automatic sinking of armed merchantmen – merely branded him as half-hearted to the increasingly vociferous right-wing lobby, which counted Ludendorff and Bauer as its firmest friends.

Bethmann-Hollweg had already told the field marshal that his government would back the submarine campaign when OHL decided it was necessary, so he must have been astonished when Ludendorff told him that he and Hindenburg might have to resign their commissions if unrestricted submarine warfare did not begin by the end of January 1917. Admiral Henning von Holtzendorf and the naval planning staffs had succeeded, in a series of meetings, in convincing the Army High Command that they could sink Allied, particularly British, shipping at such a rate that England would be brought to its knees by the middle of the year. Promising to sink 600,000 tons of shipping a month, they reckoned on eliminating 39 per cent of Britain's merchant fleet in five months, adding that 40 per cent of all neutral ships would refuse to sail to the United Kingdom. By 9 January 1917 the chancellor, still trying to delay the final decision to give him time to prepare public opinion in America on the need for ruthlessness at sea, found himself so isolated politically that even the reluctant Admiral Müller was prepared to countenance the submarine campaign 'as a last shot in the locker'. The Kaiser approved the necessary orders and insisted that OHL stop calling for the resignation of the chancellor. The head of his civil cabinet, Valentini, was so certain of the error of this decision that he wrote dramatically in his diary: 'Finis Germaniae!'

The early results of the submarine offensive were spectacular and German spirits soared accordingly. In February 1917 540,000 tons of Allied shipping was sunk; in March 600,000 tons; in April a staggering 900,000 tons. Arrivals in British ports fell from an average of 1,150 ships per month to 300. Rationing had to be tightened drastically in Great Britain and a pessimistic mood engulfed many of its leaders, military and civilian. Inevitably the United States of America was goaded into declaring war on Germany on 6 April 1917, ostensibly because of Germany's violations of international law and the loss of American ships and lives. More cynical observers noted that a defeated Entente would hardly be in a position to repay its debts to America and America was making far too great a profit from the war to let it end like that. The Germans professed no great fear of the American armed forces; their numbers would eventually be impressive but their quality was not respected, and the war would certainly be over before they could play any great part in it. Admiral Capelle boasted that his submarines would sink the American Army before it got to Europe. How ironic that not one American troopship was ever torpedoed throughout the war.

Rather it was the submarine war itself that was giving rise for alarm to German leaders. Ludendorff seems to have had an early change of heart when, in February, he warned the usually cautious Müller not to be so sure that the war would be over by August 1917. From the peak losses in April the monthly sinkings fell below the 350,000 tons mark, as the Allies organised their merchant ships into more easily protected convoys. Soon the Allies were sinking U-boats at a faster rate than they were being built and the huge claims for victory at sea came to nothing. This had a very real impact on home morale, where things were getting more and more difficult on a daily basis. The public mood would fluctuate wildly as Germany entered a period of tremendous battles, that included crushing defeats and spectacular victories.

*chapter six*

# 1917– A Year of Trials and Triumphs

Hindenburg and Ludendorff knew that the principal fighting in 1917 would be on the Western Front. They no longer felt that their head-quarters needed to be in close proximity to that of their Austro-Hungarian allies. After investigating Spa in Belgium as a possible site, the new headquarters were fixed at Kreuznach, a town close to all the main cable networks connecting to the front commands. The Germans could certainly expect a renewal of offensive action by the Entente powers in the spring. Would the British resume their attacks in Picardy or further to the north? Where would the French attack in force and where would they make diversionary efforts? When would the Italian Army attack again? Would Macedonia remain a quiet sector? How would the Turks hold on in Palestine and Mesopotamia? Could the Russians recover yet again and, with the Romanians (who were receiving a great deal of help from the French), resume offensive action in the East any time after April? A Russian attack around Mitau in January 1917 involving some heavy fighting had been an unpleasant shock.

OHL knew that the British were preparing to renew their offen-sive in Picardy in the spring of 1917, and had been concerned at the French recovery towards the end of 1916 in fighting around Verdun. One of the reasons advanced for the unrestricted submarine campaign was to disrupt the buildup of fresh divisions, arms and ammunition by the British in France. It is to the credit of the German High Command that they could take cool and rational looks at their strategic situation and make outwardly unpalatable decisions based on harsh necessity. With 154 German divisions facing 190 (usually stronger) Entente divisions on the Western Front, it was imperative that the line be shortened to release divisions into a reserve. Orders went out on 4 February that the Siegfried Line was ready for occupation and the planning stage of Operation Alberich began on 9 February. An intensive five weeks of staff work and logistical preparation followed and, on 16 March 1917, the German armies occupying the great central salient on the Western Front began an orderly retreat to their prepared positions. The skill with which the front-line troops stealthily quit their positions meant that the army was, by and large, successful in its aim of avoiding any large-scale fighting during the withdrawal. A 'devastated zone' was created behind them. Everything of any value was carted away; the population was forcibly removed back into the occupied zone; everything that might be of use to the enemy that could not be removed was destroyed. Ludendorff went to great pains in his memoirs to insist that all this grieved him and that military necessity alone dictated the German action. He is careful to explain that the poisoning of wells was forbidden, but many other booby-traps were left for the unwary enemy soldier. In particular he regretted that the sight of orchard trees hacked to the ground and the systematic demolition gave a wonderful propaganda victory to the foe, who could yet again denounce the Germans as barbaric 'Huns'. OHL would have liked to 'announce' the end of the withdrawal by a series of powerful counter-attacks from the Siegfried Line on the pursuing Allies but a realistic assessment of the condition of the German Army at that time made it inadvisable.

A valuable side benefit of the March retreat was that it seriously disrupted the plans of the Western Allies for their spring offensive. In some fighting around the middle of February troops of the Third Army had captured documents from the French 2nd Division giving detailed orders for the forthcoming attack across the Aisne River – the ambitious scheme of the new French commander, Robert Nivelle, to deliver a massive, violent blow that would rupture the German line and restore the war of movement that all Western Front generals aspired to. Ludendorff's great anxiety had been that, with their excellent lines of communication, the Entente powers could concentrate for an attack almost anywhere. With this important intelligence in his possession, he could now start to redeploy to meet the threat. With the line successfully shortened, he pulled the First Army out of the Crown Prince of Bavaria's army group, and placed it in reserve behind the troops of the Crown Prince of Prussia's army group holding the Aisne sector. The labour corps released from work on the Siegfried Line were sent down to the Aisne to begin a massive reinforcement of the defensive positions there. Training of the Western armies was even suspended for a while to allow the troops to get a good rest. Divisions were brought back from the successes in Romania, and some of the weakest Western divisions were sent to the East where things were much quieter.

The Italian front remained quiet. The Bulgarians beat off some attacks in Macedonia. The Turks won a fine defensive victory at Gaza, but their position in Mesopotamia was desperately weakened as Baghdad fell to the British on 11 March 1917. In the winter of 1916–17 the last mountain gaps in the railway link between Germany and the Turkish Empire had been completed. It was possible to send some German troops to the Middle East to stiffen Turkish resolve as part of a new Asiatic Corps under the reliable Erich von Falkenhayn, released from duties in Romania.

Hoffmann had been recording in his diary that news of disorder from the Russian interior was very encouraging, suggesting that the strain of the war would prove too much for the tsar's empire in 1917. Events began to move very quickly in March when a strike in Petrograd by Putilov factory workers escalated into bread riots by the whole populace. A clumsy attempt to deal with the strikers by a general lockout of workers produced a social explosion, the defection of the entire garrison to the side of the revolutionaries and the forming of a provisional government. Within three days the Tsar of all the Russias had abdicated and a Russian republic was born. The new government had to share authority with the local 'soviets' – committees of workers' and soldiers' delegates who wielded a great deal of practical power.

Ludendorff said that his initial reaction was that a great weight had been lifted from his chest. While the long-term situation was not at all clear, in the short term his anxieties were greatly reduced. The General Staff took the calculated decision to allow a sealed train to carry Vladimir Lenin and other major leaders of the Bolshevik faction of socialist revolutionaries through Germany on their way back to Petrograd. They did it in a deliberate attempt to spread the 'plague bacillus' of revolution through the Russian Army and body politic. Ludendorff confessed later that this was to prove fatal to Germany's true interests in the long run. But for the present he was content to be able to rotate divisions from East to West and vice versa, and his staff authorised a 'peace offensive' in the East aimed at the ordinary Russian soldier. Indeed, when *OberOst* organised a quick attack on the Stokhod River on 3 April, which easily took 10,000 highly discontented Russian prisoners, Ludendorff moved swiftly to forbid any further offensive action along the whole Eastern Front. The provisional government had reacted in an alarming fashion by forming a War Committee; that was the last thing the German High Command wanted at that time.

In April 1917 the German High Command took in their stride the declaration of war by the United States of America. As far as they were concerned America had never really been neutral and her factories had worked tirelessly to supply the Entente with arms, ammunition and equipment. It was understood that her mobilisation for war would be a protracted affair and it was hoped that the unrestricted submarine campaign would force a decision in Europe before America could

# The Western Front 1917

NORTH SEA

HOLLAND

Zeebrugge

Ostend

Nieuport

Dunkirk

Bruges

Ghent

Roulers

Ypres

Passchendaele

Messines

Lille

Calais

St Omer

Boulogne

Neuve Chapelle

Givenchy

La Bassée

Loos

Lens

Dauai

Vimy

Valenciennes

Arras

Flesquières

Cambrai

Le Cateau

Bapaume

Peronne

St Quentin

Albert

Montdidier

Noyon

La Fère

Laon

Abbeville

Somme

Amiens

Compiègne

Soissons

Rheims

Château-Thierry

Meaux

Épernay

Paris

Brussels

Liége

BELGIUM

Namur

Charleroi

Mons

Maubeuge

Landrecies

Oise

Meuse

Sambre

Mézières

Sedan

Longwy

Aisne

Verdun

St Mihiel

Marne

Seine

Oise

FRANCE

0       30 km

0       50 miles

— · — Frontiers

· · · · · · · · Limit of German Advance 1914

– – – Approximate line of the Front
from late 1914 to beginning of the
Battle of the Somme, 1 July 1916

Allied gains in 1916–17, including
ground conceded by the
Germans in early 1917

· · · · · · · · · Limit of German advance in 1918

▬▬▬ Armistice line, 11 November 1918

effectively intervene. The early results of the submarine offensive filled the German military with hope.

From the end of February Ludendorff set out from Kreuznach on a number of visits to key sectors of the Western Front, to perfect the defensive schemes of his principal commanders and formations there. The new manual for defensive fighting had been distributed and was being applied. More thinly held outpost zones were covering the main line of resistance, and counter-attack units were positioned to be able to recapture any ground lost to enemy assault. It was soon clear, from the concentration of guns, ammunition and supply dumps, and troops, that the British were planning a major attack in the Arras area. An attack by the German Sixth Army near Souchez was cancelled as part of the preparation to receive the British attack, and counter-attack divisions were moved up into a support line.

The Germans were about to get a terrible shock. The British attack on 9 April 1917, in the midst of a snow blizzard, gouged a deep penetration in the powerful new German defences. The day is famous for the storming of the Vimy Ridge by the Canadian Corps (ably supported by a British infantry brigade and British artillery), but to the south even more spectacular advances were made by British infantry divisions working in perfect harmony with devastating creeping and standing barrages, and putting into effect the new fire and movement small-unit tactics based on the new training manuals issued as a result of staff studies of the Somme fighting of the previous year.[1] Ludendorff noted especially the use of a short but intense artillery bombardment that launched the assault and the use of tanks to overcome strong points either side of the Scarpe River. He was appalled that the British attackers got in amongst the German field guns before they could be withdrawn to safety.

In his memoirs he wrote:

On that day I celebrated my birthday at Kreuznach. I had looked forward to the expected offensive with confidence, and was now deeply depressed. Was this to be the result of all our care and trouble during the past half-year? Had our principles of defensive tactics proved false, and if so what was to be done?[2]

Yet again it was Hindenburg who pulled him through his depression, grasping Ludendorff's right hand in both of his and telling him calmly that they had lived through worse crises than this and that they would win through together. Work was the great cure and so, while the battle continued, Ludendorff began an urgent analysis of the fighting and of what had gone wrong on the first day, when even a particularly good division had done very badly. He quizzed officers from the front and realised that the counter-attack divisions had been held too far back to be of any use in striking the attackers while they were still disorganised. He decided that the principles of the defence were sound and that 'the whole art of leadership lies in applying them correctly'. Under the careful direction of General Ludwig von Falkenhausen and his chief of staff, the genius of the defensive battle Colonel Lossberg, the German Sixth Army was able to absorb the further British attacks, which could never achieve again the level of overwhelming violence that carried them four miles into the enemy positions on a front of seven to nine miles. Gradually the defensive positions were restored and the fighting resumed its grimly attritional nature.

It was not long before the Germans had it confirmed to them that the British offensive was just the opening shot in a much larger plan. On 16 April a massive French attack developed against the German positions on the Chemin des Dames overlooking the Aisne Valley. The sheer violence of the assault led to some progress in terms of ground gained and prisoners taken, but the carefully prepared defences of some fine commanders and troops of the Crown Prince's armies were not greatly shaken in any fundamental way. Two days later the offensive spread into Champagne and in some hard fighting around the Moronvillers Heights, where the counter-attack divisions were committed too soon and were roughly handled, the French again made some progress. But as the battle took the normal course of Western Front actions and slowed down into a series of desperate and costly attacks and counter-attacks, it became clear that the high hopes of the French commander for a decisive breakthrough were doomed. More seriously, the French soldiery reacted bitterly to this disappointment and began to refuse orders given to them. These 'acts of collective disobedience' spread until the French Army was paralysed by mutiny. It was to the great good fortune of the Western Allies (and perhaps owes something to the good work of their intelligence organisations) that the Germans never really understood the seriousness of the situation. It is certainly true that the ability of the British to keep up the pressure in the Arras sector helped to distract the Germans from the potential prize facing them in the crippling of the French Army's offensive capability, however temporary a phenomenon that may have been.

Instead Ludendorff was recording how grateful he was that the Eastern Front was quiet and that OHL had only two major offensives to deal with at a time. Even while the fighting went on along the Scarpe, the Germans could observe that the British were shifting resources north to Flanders. The commanders, in what the Germans called the Wytschaete salient and the British called the Messines Ridge, were debating whether to evacuate back to a defensive line along the chord of the arc formed by the salient. OHL would probably have preferred a withdrawal but the local commanders, who always had a strong voice in German planning, thought that their strong positions could be held against any attack. Once again they were to suffer a crushing first-day defeat at the hands of a carefully prepared British attack. On 7 June, a day made famous by the explosion of nineteen mines that blew the top off the Messines Ridge, it was again the power and accuracy of the British artillery that crushed the defenders and allowed their infantry to sweep over what were thought to be impregnable defences. The artillery barrages destroyed any chance of German reserve formations having any influence on the battle and, by the time the battle petered out some days later, the Germans were back in the line to which they had considered withdrawing.

With some relief Ludendorff noted that the British did not exploit their victory but seemed to be pouring reinforcements of every kind into the Ypres salient further north. Having spent some months curbing the enthusiasm of *OberOst* for further attacks against the Russians, OHL now noted with alarm that the new government under Alexander Kerensky seemed to have reinvigorated the Russian Army and was firm in its resolve to stand by the Entente. Kerensky placed Brusilov in overall command of the Russian armies in the field, hoping to capitalise on the popularity of this soldiers' general. On 1 July 1917 the Russians attacked with thirty-one divisions and 1,328 guns on a fifty-mile front in Galicia. Where they struck German or Turkish troops they did not fare well, but, predictably, where they hit the Austrians they made spectacular captures of ground, prisoners and guns. When a Czech brigade in the Russian Eleventh Army came up against Austria's 19th (Czech) Division, there were wholesale desertions from the latter to the former. The presence of German troops mixed in with Austrian formations prevented a total collapse of the front as had been witnessed all too often before. With the utmost coolness, OHL quietly arranged for six divisions to be railed east from France to form the basis of a decisive counterattack. The real crisis was over by 15 July and Hoffmann was able to concentrate his force at Zborow and on the Sereth, on the northern edge of the salient created by the Russian advance. A series of Russian attacks developed in the north, around Dvinsk and Lake Narotch, but these were dealt with by local forces. On 19 July, following a hurricane bombardment organised by artillery colonel Georg Bruchmüller, nine German divisions counter-attacked the Russian Eleventh Army and put it to flight. Within a week the Russians were fleeing on a 150-mile front and the fighting lines were back on the Russo–Romanian borders.

While the Russian Army was clearly beyond all hope of causing much trouble, the Germans and their allies developed their offensive into Romania throughout August.

It was well for OHL that the military situation looked secure that summer, for the political situation reached a crisis point that must have been a grave distraction to them. For some time in Germany a right-wing coalition of ultra-conservatives, leaders of heavy industry and banking, and officers of OHL had been working to undermine the position of the Imperial Chancellor, Bethmann-Hollweg, whose efforts to keep Germany functioning as a democracy under wartime conditions had led to him being discounted as a weak and ineffectual leader with alarming tendencies towards making peace before victory. As early as January 1917 there had been calls for a strong man to save the country from certain defeat and the name of Hindenburg was mooted as both chancellor and chief of staff. While OHL would welcome the dismissal of Bethmann-Hollweg, they were perfectly aware that the soldiers could operate much more effectively with a compliant politician as chancellor. The stumbling block for them was the Kaiser's continuing good faith in Bethmann and his instinct for detecting the near-treasonous 'Bonapartist' tendencies of some of his generals and their civilian contacts. On 14 March 1917 Hindenburg asked the Kaiser directly to dismiss Bethmann and his request was refused point-blank. Hindenburg had been at odds with his emperor for some weeks over this issue and was reportedly in very low spirits.

At around Easter-time the chancellor began a process that he hoped would improve the morale of the civilian population, a serious and growing concern for all elements of the German ruling elite, by getting the Kaiser to make a speech promising a reform of the Prussian constitution and the ending of the peculiar three tier system of voting that kept the Junker class in absolute control of the State, regardless of their numbers. There was an immediate complaint from Ludendorff that OHL had not been informed of the speech in advance. (One might ask what business was it of theirs? This was indicative of the increasing expectation by officers of OHL that, in a total war, everything had a military significance and should be submitted to them for their opinion.) In private Ludendorff denounced the idea as pandering to the Russian revolution and encouraging strikes and other displays of proletarian insolence. In his memoirs Ludendorff opined that if the offer of post-war reform had been put forward in August 1914 it would have had a huge and positive effect on the national will to win. Coming when it did in 1917 he saw it as part of a 'spiritual decline' in the government and the people, as part of their loss of 'warlike ardour'.

In the Reichstag the Social Democrats seemed to be recovering something of their pre-war spirit, to the eternal vexation of OHL. Their newspaper, '*Vorwarts*', had published an article based on a resolution of the Party Committee calling for independent State institutions, sympathy with the aims of the Russian revolution, and for a peace without annex-ations. Hindenburg immediately went to the Kaiser to denounce this further example of the inability of the imperial chancellor to control the parties in the Reichstag, and to renew his demand for Bethmann's dismissal forthwith. It was Valentini, the head of the Kaiser's civil cabinet, who reminded his emperor that Bethmann was still popular in the country, with a particularly large following in south Germany.

Ludendorff had already devised a scheme to put the chancellor on the spot by openly encouraging a public discussion of war aims, to which his friends in the right-wing, Pan-German press responded with alacrity. Bethmann-Hollweg explained that he did not want this debate in public because he still aspired to driving a wedge between some of the Entente powers and encouraging at least one of them into a separate peace. German society was divided between those who had vested interests in securing profit from the war, together with those with strong ideologi-cal motivation towards seeing a greater, stronger Germany emerge from the struggle, and those large sections of people who saw only suffering and hardship, and who would welcome a peace at any price. The question of Germany's right to annexe any or all of the conquered territories was often the point of difference between these two contending views. The split on this issue was not always obvious. On the Western Front, Crown Prince Rupert of Bavaria was a known advocate of a 'peace of understanding' to end the war soon; in the East, Hoffmann sought only 'a reasonable peace'. But the Pan-German, heavy industry bloc most closely associated with OHL made huge demands on Poland, Romania, Serbia, the Baltic states, Belgium and parts of France.

The fate of conquered Poland had long been a source of feuding between OHL and the chancellor, and increasingly between Germany and Austria-Hungary. Ever since 1915 Ludendorff had planned to create an independent Polish state, detached from Russia and in alliance with Germany. Bethmann-Hollweg planned a large Poland as part of a post-war settlement; Ludendorff wanted a smaller state immediately, along the lines of Napoleon's Grand Duchy of Warsaw, which he hoped would be the recruiting ground for Polish divisions to serve alongside the German Army on the Eastern Front. Once again OHL insisted that Poland was a purely military problem that they should be allowed to settle in their own way. Late in 1916 the German military governor of Poland published appeals for volunteers to serve in a Polish army for which there was no clear national territory, no government, no constitution and no ruler. As Germany was busily deporting Polish workers to its own factories, it should surprise no one that, far from flocking to the colours, the Poles were soon demonstrating against these absurd calls. The placards read, 'No government, no army'. The scheme fizzled out by April 1917 when only 4,700 recruits had come forward instead of the five divisions hoped for.

Austria-Hungary responded to these German moves by declaring that Austrian Poland (Galicia) would achieve full autonomy under the empire. Hindenburg was particularly incensed at this and wrote a very strong note to the imperial chancellor in which he expressed the exasperation that many German leaders felt towards their ally:

> ... by not interfering in the internal affairs of Austria-Hungary before
> the war and during the war, our conduct of the war has constantly
> been made more difficult. If we continue to be afraid of such inter-
> ference in an area where our interests are directly at stake, we will
> give up all hope of strengthening Austria-Hungary and the question
> arises then why we are still fighting for Austria at all.[3]

The chancellor reminded the field marshal that talk like that would drive Austria-Hungary into a separate peace. Germany already knew that the new Austrian emperor had sounded out France about possible terms early in 1917. While OHL made new demands that Polish formations should take an oath of allegiance to the Kaiser, the leaders of the Russian revolution dangled the prospect of complete independence before the Polish people, which generated a wave of anti-German strikes. By August 1917 the exasperated OHL transferred the tiny Polish Legion to the Austrian Army and busied itself with other things.

The chancellor and OHL had also clashed over the policy towards Belgium. The former pursued a strongly pro-Fleming line in an attempt to gain their active co-operation with German war aims. The latter wanted an increasing role in the total exploitation of the country, its resources and its labour force. Since September 1915 the Germans had been deporting Belgian workers to German factories, keeping them in squalid work camps. This had incensed the Americans in particular, and a large number of American charities were involved in succouring 'gallant little Belgium'. Ludendorff was convinced that these charities made the Belgian workers reluctant to 'volunteer' for war service in the Reich. Hindenburg and Ludendorff made similar representations to the German government. Hindenburg said, 'In my opinion all political considerations have to be ignored in the light of our own desperate situation'; Ludendorff: 'Social and legal considerations should be regarded as secondary'. Bethmann resisted this line stoutly, and the German military governor of Belgium, General Bissing, was also reluctant to take measures that would only make the Belgians more difficult to manage. Hindenburg demanded of him: 'The still rich economic resources of Belgium should be sued for the good of our war effort'. Under the labour requirements of the Hindenburg programme Belgium was to supply 200,000 extra workers for German war factories. In fact these were rounded up and dispatched so quickly that there was not sufficient work found for them and a great deal of unnecessary suffering occurred which did enormous propaganda damage to Germany in America. It was not enough that Ludendorff thought 'the conscription of workmen for Germany was in the interest of the Belgians themselves, since unemployment had reached a high figure'.[4] Belgium remained another battleground between a German government trying to conduct 'normal' political life on the world stage and a military leadership intent on bringing every aspect of national life under its control in order to prosecute the war more effectively.

To try and curb this feuding the Kaiser called for a conference at Kreuznach on 23 April 1917 attended by Bethmann-Hollweg and representatives of the Foreign Office, and the leaders of OHL. The latter arrived with a most comprehensive and maximalist set of demands, backed up with all the necessary maps and draft proposals. Germany would annexe Courland and Lithuania, and several islands in the Baltic, together with 'buffer strips' along the Silesian borders; Poland would be expanded to the east under German military government; Russia would be compensated in Galicia and Moldavia; Austria would be compensated in Romania and Serbia; Serbia, Montenegro and Albania would form a Slavic state within the Austro-Hungarian Empire; Germany would have 'rights' (for which read total control) in Romanian oilfields; Bulgaria would regain the Dobruja (from Romania) but Germany would have control of the Black Sea Railway; Belgium would remain under occupation until a final peace conference, but Liège, the coast down to Bruges and the Arlon iron-ore mines would be annexed, and Belgian railways would remain under German management; the Longwy-Briey iron-ore mines would be annexed and France compensated for them. The question of the Balkans, Asia Minor, naval bases and colonies could all be settled at a later date.

The chancellor privately considered this programme a complete fantasy to which the Entente powers would never agree. However he now accepted that his own moderate foreign policy had been unsuccessful, the submarine campaign seemed to be going well and he thought it best to go along with the military leaders in their bid to win the war in 1917. It was a complete victory for OHL over the civilian government in terms of national foreign policy aims. The Austrians were invited to Kreuznach in May and the whole programme was forced upon them. Hindenburg explained to them that his approach to a post-war settlement was framed entirely with the firm conviction that England would use any peace settlement as the basis for a renewed attack on Germany almost at once. He wanted to create a 'fortress Germany' that would be equipped and able to fight another three-year war against the hated English enemy. Over 17–18 May the Austrians agreed to Germany controlling Romania's oilfields and Salonika and its railway lines into the interior, and to having a naval base at Valona and an economic base at Constanţa on the Black Sea. The Kreuznach Programme was hailed as another OHL triumph, and any falling away from it would be held up as examples of the weakness of Bethmann-Hollweg's government and their inability to support Germany's armed forces in their great struggle. Within days Austria was making those new proposals about the future of Poland already discussed above which suggested that, far from settling foreign policy, Kreuznach was something of a false dawn of peace.

Hindenburg had been trying to galvanise the imperial chancellor to rally the war-spirit of the nation. In an exchange of letters he warned against overly optimistic assessments of the submarine campaign and of the implacable hostility of the Entente powers. On 19 June 1917 he wrote to Bethmann-Hollweg:

These dangers are undoubtedly recognised by clear-thinking people among our enemies. If in spite of this they advocate continuation of the war, it is because they expect the collapse of Germany and her allies to take place before their own. It may be that they hope to bring about this collapse by a victory on land, but they rely far more on economic and political causes, such as food difficulties, shortage of raw materials, disunion, discontent, and the supremacy of the German Radical Social Democracy. They base this expectation on the waning of our power of resistance at home, the growth of international sentiments, the state of our food supply, and the longing for peace to which we unfortunately give expression so often.

A revival of our internal strength would be the most potent means of persuading our enemies of the futility of prolonging the war until their own means of existence are in danger of destruction. On the other hand, every complaint of disappointed hopes, every sign of exhaustion and longing for peace on our part or that of our allies, any talk of the alleged impossibility of standing another winter campaign, can only have the effect of prolonging the war.[5]

Bethmann–Hollweg's reply was frank and depressing. He admitted that he found it hard to summon up the energy to act decisively and that he feared a 'helot's peace' rather than a peace of understanding, because of David Lloyd George's utter hostility to Germany. On 27 June Hindenburg wrote to the Kaiser suggesting, yet again, that it was time for the chancellor to go:

Our greatest anxiety at this moment, however, is the decline in the national spirit. It must be revived, or we shall lose the war. Even our allies need a powerful tonic, otherwise there is a danger of their deserting us. For this it is necessary to solve those economic problems which are the most difficult and are of the greatest importance for the future .... The question arises whether the Chancellor is capable of solving these problems – and they must be correctly solved, or we are lost![6]

The political crisis came to a head in July 1917. It was precipitated by a Centre Party member of the German parliament, Matthias Erzberger, who had already caused an upset with OHL back in April. At that time he had gone to the Socialist peace conference in Stockholm, with his government's cynical blessing, and had got so carried away with his good relations with the representatives of Russia that he had entered into armistice talks with them which included highly detailed proposals of a strictly military nature. Although Ludendorff had known a good deal about this meeting, and had agreed to attempts to suborn the chief Russian negotiator, OHL flew into a perfect rage when the armistice was suggested and made it the basis of yet another attack on the chancellor for completely failing to control the country's foreign policy. This was at the time of the Kreuznach conference on war aims and added to the general atmosphere of civilian incompetence that resulted in OHL's triumph there.

Then, on 6 July 1917, Erzberger stood up at a meeting of the Central Committee of the Reichstag and delivered a stunningly honest speech. He declared that the expectation of victory based on an unrestricted submarine campaign was 'perfectly hopeless', that there was no chance of Germany winning the war, that Germany's allies were in an even more parlous state than she was herself and that Germany should seek peace without conquests immediately. The Reichstag deputies had been sheltered from such unpalatable truths and there is the hint that Erzberger got his 'insider' information from the highly political and scheming right-winger, Colonel Bauer, who was presumably looking to create a crisis to break the power of the chancellor. War Minister Stein at once telephoned OHL and invited Hindenburg and Ludendorff to Berlin to seek an audience with the Kaiser to discuss 'home affairs'. They arrived the next day to be lectured by the Kaiser on their impudence at interfering in domestic political matters that were of no concern to them whatsoever. The War Minister tried to deny that he had called them to Berlin for that purpose but the chancellor produced a copy of a cable showing that he had indeed suggested the visit and was making matters worse by his denials. They were ordered to return to their headquarters forthwith. Colonel Bauer was able to tell Erzberger that a proper discussion of his concerns was being blocked by Bethmann-Hollweg and that Ludendorff was the true champion of free speech in the Reichstag against the repressive Bethmann-Hollweg; a curious reversal of roles if ever there was one. On their return to OHL, Hindenburg and Ludendorff cabled to the Kaiser that the army's fighting power was being undermined by talk of a peace without annexations.

The massed forces of German conservatism could sense a victory and stepped up the pressure in many different ways. On 8 July 1917 the Prussian Ministry of State flatly rejected the electoral reforms that had been proposed by the chancellor. Bethmann-Hollweg offered his resignation to the Kaiser but Wilhelm stood by his man and would not accept it. Admiral Müller could see how things were going and recorded in his diary for 9 July, 'What an irony of Fate! The Chancellor ... is falling a victim to the High Command, to the Hindenburg-Ludendorff team whom he once placed firmly in the saddle ...'. The Prussian Crown Prince came to Berlin on leave and tried to persuade his father of the correctness of the OHL position but the Kaiser, backed by Valentini, assured him that any sudden changes in the government would be unwise. The next day, 12 July, Colonel Bauer set up a meeting between the Crown Prince and Reichstag party leaders for the simple purpose of denouncing the imperial chancellor in the fiercest possible terms, ending with a declaration that his resignation was essential if Germany was to bring the war to a successful conclusion. Bethmann-Hollweg tried to confront Ludendorff directly by asking if he was using the threat of resignation to undermine his position and Ludendorff gave a positively Delphic reply: 'I have not ordered any officer to tell any member of the Reichstag that I can no longer work with the Chancellor von Bethmann-Hollweg'.[7]

Bethmann-Hollweg tried to continue with the work of government and passed to Hindenburg the text of a peace resolution being discussed in the Reichstag. The field marshal was stunned at this 'peace of renunciation' and insisted on this vital clause being removed: 'Forcible seizure of territory and political, economic or financial acts of force are not commensurate with such a peace'. This time the Kaiser backed his generals forcefully against the chancellor. Hindenburg and Ludendorff both announced their intention to resign, infuriating the Kaiser who saw it as a blatant attempt to blackmail him. To end the crisis the Kaiser was obliged to accept the chancellor's resignation.

Hindenburg and Ludendorff addressed members of the Reichstag on that very day on the war situation. They said that on land the situation was serious but secure, that the supply position, especially of ammunition, was improving and that the Americans were not an immediate threat. The results of the submarine campaign were not decisive but it would continue. They strongly denounced the peace resolution as injurious to the morale of the army and the people. Their message was that victory was assured if the army was backed by a united people. At one stage Ludendorff suggested that no great offensive from any of the combatants would end the war but that the complete demoralisation of the Entente was imminent. Hindenburg had sent a message to the so-called Independent Committee (a Pan-German front organisation) saying, 'The times are grave but victory is certain'.

There was a marked reluctance among German politicians of stature to step into the chancellor's shoes and so it came to pass that the harmless Georg Michaelis assumed the position. 'With God's help I will give it a try', was his tentative reply to the offer of the post (which was almost certainly suggested by the Kaiser's aide, and 'OHL agent', Colonel General Hans von Plessen). Michaelis had been head of the Wartime Food Office and had dined at OHL to discuss food matters sufficiently often to be seen by them as a friend and ally. Hindenburg and Ludendorff gave him their immediate and strong backing. A jovial Ludendorff

ABOVE LEFT General Erich Ludendorff (1865–1937): the mercurial 'workaholic' who finally broke under the strain of total war. (AKG)

ABOVE RIGHT Field Marshal Paul von Beneckendorf und von Hindenburg (1847–1934): a massive calming influence on the Great General Staff, the army and the nation. (AKG)

BELOW Colonel (later Major General) Max Hoffmann (1869–1927): the mischievous genius of High Command, East. (AKG)

ABOVE LEFT General Alfred Count von Schlieffen (1833–1913): Chief of the Great General Staff 1891–1906, whose strategy for a war on two fronts formed the basis of the 1914 campaigns. (AKG)

ABOVE RIGHT Chancellor Theobald von Bethmann-Hollweg (1851–1921): the most senior victim of Great General Staff political interference. (AKG)

BELOW Hindenburg, Kaiser Wilhelm II and Ludendorff discussing the war situation at Pless in 1917. (AKG)

ABOVE LEFT General Erich von Falkenhayn (1861–1922): War Minister and Chief of the Great General Staff, replaced by Hindenburg in 1916. (AKG)

ABOVE RIGHT Lieutenant General Adolf Wild von Hohenborn (1860–1925): Director of the *Kriegsamt* and Prussian War Minister, 'first blood' to the political machinations of the Great General Staff. (Ullstein)

BELOW LEFT Georg Michaelis (1857–1936): the Great General Staff's choice as Chancellor to replace Bethmann-Hollweg – a short-lived appointment! (AKG)

BELOW RIGHT Gottlieb von Jagow (1863–1935): a State Secretary at the Foreign Office who proved 'unacceptable' to the Great General Staff. (AKG)

TOP LEFT German infantry in action during the First Battle of the
Masurian Lakes, September 1914: a typical view of early entrenchments
soon to be replaced by more substantial and scientifically designed
defences. (Ullstein)

BOTTOM LEFT Restoring the war of movement: thoroughly modern-
looking German infantry of 18th Army attacking between Montdidier
and Noyon, June 1918. (AKG)

ABOVE A pre-war view of a Krupp's armaments factory: a powerful
and confident nation preparing for war. (AKG)

ABOVE A strike in August 1917 at the Leuna works in Saxony–Anhalt: a hungry and discontented work force wanting an end to the war. (Ullstein)

BELOW The blockade bites deep. In 1917 Berlin housewives are reduced to exchanging potato peel for firewood: coal for domestic use was a thing of the past. (Ullstein)

ABOVE Jubilant French crowds greet British troops marching into Lille in October 1918: a stage in the 'Hundred Days' offensive that ended the war with victory for the Entente powers. (Mary Evans Library)

BELOW 11 November 1918: signing the Armistice on Marshal Foch's railway train in the Compiègne Forest. (Corbis)

ABOVE Revolutionary sailors, soldiers and workers under the Red
Flag: the Great General Staff's worst nightmare manifests itself in
Berlin, November 1918. (AKG)

BELOW On the brink of civil war: the revolutionary sailor, Tost,
addresses the crowd at the funeral of sailors killed in Berlin street
fighting, December 1918. (AKG)

even helped the deputy Scheidemann to draft a new peace resolution, in which the Social Democrat was persuaded of the necessity of various territorial acquisitions, and this satisfactory peace feeler quickly passed through the Reichstag on 19 July, with Michaelis cleverly agreeing to it 'subject to his own interpretation'. OHL could now celebrate a new and compliant chancellor and an utterly meaningless Reichstag peace resolution.

With this victory against 'the enemy within' OHL moved to strengthen its grip. First Hindenburg sent a long memorandum to Chancellor Michaelis explaining the reasons why OHL had insisted on the removal of Bethmann-Hollweg. His feeble foreign policy and failure to consult closely with OHL were high on the list but it also included his dithering over the start of the submarine campaign, the whole fiasco over the governance of Poland, his poor record on the future of Belgium, his failure to mobilise the people and the economy for total war, his poor record as a propagandist, his failure to control strikes and the damage he caused to the prestige of the monarchy. It is hard not to see this memo as a stark warning to Michaelis on the fate of chancellors who do not follow the OHL line.

The rampant right went on to create the new Fatherland Party, under the leadership of Admiral Tirpitz and Wolfgang Kapp, which was the OHL's direct mouthpiece in the Reichstag. It is somewhat disingenuous of Ludendorff to insist in his memoirs that he had no connection with this organisation but he did record how disappointed he was that they seemed to degenerate into another squabbling party much like all the others. In despair Ludendorff wrote, 'The Lord in Heaven forsook His German people, because it had forsaken itself'.

OHL also proceeded to take a grip on the moral well-being of the nation through their Programme for Patriotic Instruction. After a particularly alarmist report on the work of socialist agitators in the ranks of the army, the Intelligence Section of OHL under Colonel Nicolai had already proposed a programme of lectures for the field army to improve

morale and the understanding of the war and its purpose. Both
Hindenburg and Ludendorff had been giving a great deal of thought
to this problem and Nicolai's suggestions were timely. This 'work of
enlightenment among the troops' was necessary because of the strains
the prolonged war was putting on the army. Ludendorff wrote in
support of Nicolai's ideas:

> The German Army, owing to the spirit that animates it, is superior to
> its enemies, and a powerful support to its Allies.
>
> At the beginning of the war the foundations of this spirit were
> enthusiasm and the discipline that had been inculcated during pro-
> longed peace training. The three years of war have changed and
> enlarged these foundations. A comprehensible longing for home,
> family, and calling, may weaken its war resolution and take the edge
> off the will to hold out till the final victory is gained.
>
> The long duration of the war has also brought with it want and
> sacrifice in increasing measure, both at home and in the Army. The
> more these burdens oppress the spirit of the Army, the more must the
> foundations of fighting power be laid on conviction, sense of duty
> and definite resolve. To supply this need is the task of patriotic instruc-
> tion in the Army.

On 15 September 1917 he expanded his ideas on the subject:

> The enemy's determination to destroy us and the necessity for us to
> go on fighting are less obvious to the troops employed on the lines
> of communication, on garrison duty and at home, than to the fighting
> forces themselves. For this reason special attention must be given to the
> morale of the troops on the lines of communication, and patriotic
> instruction must be especially fostered among them.
>
> The proper course is to concentrate on the relationship between
> the home and the Army. From the spiritual point of view and for the
> fulfilment of the national tasks, the people and the Army are one.

Consequently, great importance attaches to the cultivation of patriotic feeling among the people at home, a duty which is carried on in conjunction with the civil authorities. The prosecution of this task must be regarded as one of the most important duties of the military authorities at home.[8]

OHL, with the active co-operation of the War Ministry, delivered the programme to the entire nation. 'Political officers' lectured to the troops; Ludendorff invited a Lieutenant Schmetzer to give to the General Staff at Kreuznach exactly the same talk (on the consequences for the workers of a German defeat – a new slavery to international capitalism) he would deliver to the front-line fighters. Ludendorff was so pleased that he sent Schmetzer on to Berlin to lecture some government ministers in the same way. The district and fortress commanders made the same talks available to civilians in their areas. The lectures covered the economic progress of Germany before 1914, the causes of the war and the dire consequences of losing the war, especially as it would affect the working class. The war was described as a struggle between two great wills, and it was stressed that, without common unity, the future was bleak. This smoothly went on to categorise all strikers as enemies of the people, whose action was paid for with the blood of the soldiers. As the lectures were free of party politics the Reichstag gave its approval in October 1917, but Ludendorff noted acidly that the army received 'not the slightest assistance from the civil authorities'.

The distractions of high politics and the economy continued to absorb the attention of the Army High Command throughout the year. OHL decided that General Groener at the *Kriegsamt* was too soft on the demands of labour and Ludendorff promptly reassigned him to the command of an infantry division on the Western Front. It was not long before War Minister Stein was authorising the most brutal military suppression of strikes in Silesia, and this was followed by denunciations of the workers' councils and their 'obsession' with controlling war profits.

The Auxiliary Service Law had proved a failure and Hindenburg resorted to demanding the fullest possible implementation of the Law of the State of Siege. Michaelis and his ministers resisted this as being politically divisive.

When Pope Benedict XV made a new peace proposal in August 1917, with its special reference to a free Belgium, Chancellor Michaelis received it favourably and tried to interest OHL in moderating their demands on that country in particular. This was the fatal moment when OHL decided that the mild Michaelis was no longer 'their man'. Hindenburg sent a strongly worded letter explaining that the navy would require the annexation of the Belgian coast, and that the country and its economy would have to remain under German administration for many years to come, an expansion of his firm view that another war with England was inevitable. Ludendorff's memo insisted that the Central Powers were now stronger than the Entente and that, by the end of 1917, they would be in a position to make peace proposals that would include huge gains in the East and German occupation of Belgium, and 'control' of Holland and Denmark. Through its political forces in the Reichstag OHL proceeded to destroy Michaelis's prestige. By 22 October the Reichstag was voting to have him replaced by a more reforming chancellor. Once again the Prussian Crown Prince conveyed to his father the strong opinion of OHL and heavy industry that a more co-operative chancellor was needed. The Kaiser asked the Bavarian president, Count Hertling, to become imperial chancellor and Michaelis resigned on 1 November. While Hindenburg had a strong personal dislike for Hertling, a south German and a Catholic to boot, and would have liked to have been consulted more on the new appointee, OHL did (once again) get a replacement when it wanted and Hertling did pledge to work in harmony with them.

Meanwhile the war on the Western Front reached new heights of ferocity. The series of battles in Flanders in the autumn of 1917, known officially by the British as Third Ypres and forever etched in popular memory by the doomladen name of Passchendaele, are generally remembered as demonstrating the ultimate in First World War futility and stupidity. The image of mud-filled craters, the high casualty lists and the relatively small gains of ground all combined to label this as a British disaster. Ironically the Germans saw the fighting in exactly the same light.

'The fighting on the Western Front became more severe and costly than any the German army had yet experienced', Ludendorff wrote.[9] The responsibility for handling the battle while so many troops were still tied down in the East weighed heavily upon him: 'It shook even me'. His attention had been devoted to Hoffmann's plans to move troops by rail from Galicia north for an attack at Riga, followed by a complex and speedy redeployment back to Moldavia for a blow in the south. On 31 July 1917, a huge bombardment (the heaviest ever seen on the Western Front to date) preceded the British attack on Pilckem Ridge, heralding for Ludendorff 'a long period of tremendous anxiety'. What seemed like early success for the attackers soon collapsed. The progress of the attack was broken up by the deep German defences, with their mutually supporting pillboxes, and then was halted and often forced back by powerful counter-attacks organised by Fourth Army's chief of staff, Colonel Lossberg. This almost perfect application of the defence manual was somewhat overshadowed by the break in the weather that ushered in the worst period of rainfall in north-west Europe for seventy-five years. Having completely lost the momentum that usually accompanied a powerful first-day attack, the British battle commander, Sir Hubert Gough, persisted in battering away along his chosen lines of attack. Actions on 10, 16 and 19–24 August were, in the main, dreary failures for a rain-sodden and exhausted British Army and British morale sunk lower at this period than at any other time in the war. At the daily meetings with the Kaiser both Hindenburg and Ludendorff were able to express their confidence in the ability of the Western armies to hold their positions. Ludendorff rarely mentioned the weather as a factor but did comment on the relentless nature of the fighting and the rising losses. He was more alarmed at the seizure of Hill 70 near Lens by the Canadian Corps, and at signs of French recovery in attacks on the Aisne and at Verdun.

As things quietened down slightly in Flanders, there were other concerns. Ludendorff himself was involved in a bad railway accident that shook him physically. Then he received the news that his much-loved eldest stepson, a pilot in the German Air Force, had been shot down over the English Channel and was presumed killed. (His body would be washed ashore in Holland some weeks later.) Yet another Italian attack on the Isonzo front (the eleventh battle of that name) had pressed the Austrians so hard that they were forced to send troops to Italy from Moldavia, thus ruining yet another German offensive scheme in the East. It was as a result of this that Ludendorff set his OHL planners to looking at a way to strike at Italy and relieve their ailing Austrian ally. With things relatively quiet in the West, the Germans were able to withdraw a division and a brigade of cyclists from the Flanders garrison and send them east where they would be trained for amphibious warfare prior to seizing some important islands in the Baltic. This operation was made possible by the clinically efficient attack made by General Oskar von Hutier's troops at Riga on 1 September 1917. These soldiers had been trained in the most advanced infantry tactics and co-operated with a barrage organised by the artillery genius, Colonel Georg Bruch-müller. The improved situation in the East meant that other divisions could be sent to the West, where carefully selected attack formations were in turn released for service in Italy. OHL was greatly focused on these developments when a new crisis loomed in Flanders.

A change in the British approach to the battle there was to have dire effects on the German defenders. Sir Douglas Haig had decided to give overall command of the Flanders offensive to General Sir Herbert Plumer. While he might have approved of the larger vision of the 'thruster' Gough, Haig recognised that the battle needed to develop under the more careful management of 'Daddy' Plumer. Plumer had commanded the Second Army guarding the Ypres salient since May 1915 and knew it better than any man in the British Army. He and his staff had made important deductions from the nature of the current fighting and Haig agreed to the temporary halting of attacks while Plumer organised a powerful new blow against the strongest portion of the German line. This time divisions were given strictly limited objectives on narrow attack frontages, and were supported by the highest ratio of guns to front attacked ever seen in the war to date. Artillery bombardments of the most intricate nature were designed to suppress enemy defences and supporting artillery, walk the infantry onto their objectives and, most importantly, the positions won were then to be immediately prepared for defence. The predicted and predictable German counter-attacks were then to be destroyed by devastating artillery and machine-gun barrages organised well in advance of the battle. Plumer had prepared four such set piece battles that would gouge out sections of the German positions on the ridge overlooking Ypres, from which the British could not be evicted.

The battle of the Menin Road Ridge on 20 September 1917 was a clinical British victory, won in a period of heat and dust that hardly fits the popular image of the campaign. Ludendorff immediately recognised this new and dangerous development in the attack method of his enemy:

> After a period of profound quiet in the West, which led to some hope that the Battle of Flanders was over, another terrific assault was made on our lines on 20 September. The third bloody act of the battle had begun. The main force of the attack was directed against the Passchendaele–Gheluvelt line. Obviously the English were trying to gain the high ground between Ypres and the Roulers–Menin line, which affords an extensive view in both directions. These heights were also exceptionally important for us, as they afforded us ground observation posts and a certain amount of cover from hostile view.

Ludendorff is making the natural point here, often misunderstood by armchair critics, that in a battle so dominated by artillery assets, the fight to obtain or retain any observation point of advantage to the artillery assumed the highest importance. Grievous infantry losses for seemingly negligible 'heights' could have the greatest impact on the course of the current and all subsequent battles:

> The enemy's onslaught on the 20th was successful, which proved the superiority of the attack over the defence .... The power of the attack lay in the artillery, and in the fact that ours did not do enough damage to the hostile infantry as they were assembling, and, above all, at the actual time of the assault ... the 26th proved a day of heavy fighting, accompanied by every circumstance that could cause us loss. We might be able to stand the loss of ground, but the reduction of our fighting strength was again all the heavier. Once more we were involved in a terrific struggle in the West, and had to prepare for a continuation of the attacks on many parts of the front.[10]

The aim to defend 'lightly' and to recover lost ground by counter-attack was playing into the hands of the British and leading to the loss of important artillery observation posts and irreplaceable losses amongst the veteran infantry. At the audience with the Kaiser on 30 September Admiral Müller reported that Ludendorff maintained: 'that the latest British attacks – artillery barrage, smoke and machine-gun fire against our massed divisions on a comparatively narrow front – are almost irresistible'.[11]

The analysts at OHL were hard at work in their search for a solution to the tactical problem:

> After each attack I discussed the tactical experiences with General von Kuhl and Colonel von Lossberg, sometimes at the Front, sometimes on the telephone. This time I again went to Flanders in order to talk over the same questions with officers who had taken part in the

fighting. Our defensive tactics had to be developed further, somehow or other. We were all agreed on that. The only thing was, it was so infinitely difficult to hit on the right remedy. We could only proceed by careful experiment. The proposals of the officers on the spot tended rather in the direction of our former tactics; they amounted to a slight, but only a slight, reinforcement of our front lines, and the abandonment of the counter-attack by the counter-attack divisions, local counter-attacks being substituted for this. These local counter-attacks were to be made by a division in the second line, to be brought close up and spread over a wide front, before the enemy's attack began. So, while the front line was to be held rather more densely once more, in order to gain in power, the whole battlefield was to be given more depth than ever. GHQ would thus, generally speaking, have to provide a second division for every fighting division in the front line, an unheard-of expenditure of force. That the deployment of a second division in rear of practically every one in the front line would increase the power of the defence was a simple sum of arithmetic. But the second sum was equally simple; that our lines on other fronts would have to be thinned out even more than they had been hitherto. I said I would see what I could do. I agreed to the tactical changes, although misgivings were expressed among my Staff at this departure from the 'Defensive Battle'. I thought I ought to give way to the experience of the officers at the front.

Another tactical detail which was emphasised everywhere was the value of ground observation for artillery. Only by that means could the attacking hostile infantry be annihilated, particularly after penetrating our front, or fire be concentrated on decisive points of the battlefield.[12]

Plumer continued his remorseless series of limited offensives and, on his third step, inflicted a grievous defeat on the German troops opposed to him. It is ironic that this battle of Broodseinde (4 October

1917) was used by David Lloyd George in his memoirs as a sarcastic euphemism for a bogus victory claimed by Haig and his GHQ, when Ludendorff and OHL considered it one of the 'black days' of the German Army on the Western Front:

> Early in October the artillery action revived, and on the 2nd and 3rd artillery engagements of great violence took place. The infantry battle commenced on the morning of the 4th. It was extraordinarily severe, and again we only came through it with enormous loss. It was evident that the idea of holding the front line more densely, adopted at my last visit to the front in September, was not the remedy. I now followed my own judgement without asking for further outside opinions, and recommended the 4th Army to form an advanced zone, that is to say, a narrow strip between the enemy's front line and the line which our troops were to hold by mobile defence. The enemy would have to cross this strip in making his attack, and our artillery would have time to get on to him before he could reach our main line of resistance. The great difficulty lay in withdrawing the garrison of the advanced zone in case of attack, and in bringing the artillery barrage back to our own line. The term 'advanced zone' had been defined in various ways, and the ideas often became confused. The principle of it was simple. The 4th Army complied with my suggestion somewhat reluctantly, and did not accept it with conviction for some time. I never ceased to lay stress on the principles of the employment of artillery in masses and the utmost possible concentration of artillery fire.[13]

The relentless fighting in early and mid October put a tremendous strain on the German armies in the West, where more and more divisions were being rotated through the battle. After commenting on the remarkably high 'wastage' in Flanders, Ludendorff stated quite bluntly: 'In the West we began to be short of troops'. Some troops earmarked for the East and for Italy had to be returned to France and Flanders. As the Canadian Corps arrived in theatre to carry the offensive up onto the Passchendaele Ridge in one last, exhausting and rain-sodden series of attacks, Ludendorff writes some moving descriptions of the suffering of the German soldier and his defensive triumphs:

> Enormous masses of ammunition, such as the human mind had never imagined before the war, were hurled upon the bodies of men who passed a miserable existence scattered about in mud-filled shell-holes. The horror of the shell-hole area of Verdun was surpassed. It was no longer life at all. It was mere unspeakable suffering. And through this world of mud the attackers dragged themselves, slowly, but steadily, and in dense masses. Caught in the advanced zone by our hail of fire they often collapsed, and the lonely man in the shell-hole breathed again. Then the mass came on again. Rifle and machine-gun jammed with the mud. Man fought against man, and only too often was the mass successful.[14]

He described his British enemy as charging 'like a wild bull at the iron wall which kept him from our submarine bases'. His principal worry was that the truly heroic resistance of the front-line fighters would be simply ground down by the unrelenting pressure: '…and yet it must be admitted that certain units no longer triumphed over the demoralising effects of the defensive battle as they had done formerly'. When the British attacks finally ended on 10 November there was a pronounced sense of relief. The German High Command reported to their Kaiser on what they considered to be a defensive victory of great importance. Ludendorff had already begun a planning process for 1918 to make sure that his Western armies would not have to endure such a trial again.

Two further triumphs were to be recorded by German arms before the year ended. At two o'clock in the morning of a misty and rainy 24 October a hurricane bombardment crashed down upon the Italian positions along the upper reaches of the Isonzo, in the mountains around Caporetto. After four hours of shelling, of which nearly half was gas, the Italian artillery was silenced and the German Fourteenth Army launched an attack with ten Austro–German divisions on a twenty-mile front. Penetrating swiftly along the valleys they advanced fourteen miles and put three Italian divisions to flight. Next day the elite *Alpenkorps* seized more vital mountain peaks and ridges and the Italian position was cracked wide open. By 27 October the leading German troops were at Cividale, threatening the rear of the whole Italian Army defending the Isonzo. General Cadorna had ordered a full-scale retreat of the Italian Army, Britain was pulling troops out of the Ypres offensive for urgent redeployment to Italy and the French had dispatched four divisions and an army headquarters. As the total of prisoners passed the 100,000 mark the Austrians and Germans forced the line of the Tagliamento on 4 November and kept up their pursuit of the fleeing Italian Army towards the River Piave. With dire warnings of Italy being forced to sue for a separate peace, the Entente powers sent all the troops and guns they could spare to Italy, under such senior commanders as Plumer and Fayolle. With such tangible support the Italian Army was able to rally itself to a remarkable degree and bring the pursuit to a halt along the line of the Piave.

Once again the insertion of a few veteran German divisions into an unexpected part of the line and the execution of a well-planned, violent assault at a key point had brought about a spectacular collapse of their enemy. But again, after stunning initial success, the distances covered, the need to repair railways and advance the railheads, and the inevitable slowing of the momentum of the attack meant that the offensive did not achieve the ultimate prize of putting one of the Entente powers out of the war. Ludendorff could be justifiably proud of the achievement: 'German leadership and German troops had gained fresh laurels, and given further proofs of their superiority in the war of movement. On occasion our full force had not been developed owing to incidents arising from the lack of experience of young troops'.[15] This was a further admission that, despite numerous victories accruing to her, Germany was getting towards the end of her resources.

For a few days in November it looked as if another crisis was at hand in France. During the Ypres fighting Ludendorff had often referred to the use by the British of tanks. He could be generally dismissive of them as the terrain and weather conditions did not favour their use to any great extent. He chided his front-line fighters for their 'tank fright' and assured them that a steady nerve would see the cumbersome and slow machines dealt with by German artillery. On 20 November the British showed for the first time what could be achieved by the mass use of tanks in a surprise attack, supported by the massed use of artillery firing an entirely 'predicted' hurricane bombardment. Julian Byng's Third Army, backed by 389 tanks, broke into an extremely strong portion of the Hindenburg Line near Cambrai, capturing more prisoners than they had total casualties. The Germans were fortunate that a division from the East had just detrained at Cambrai and was able to enter the fray immediately. The swift marshalling of reserves to the area, coupled with the fact that the British were not really ready to exploit the success of what had originally been thought of as a 'raid' on the enemy positions, saw the battle quickly degenerate into the usual attritional struggle. By 30 November Germany had brought up well-trained counter-attack forces under the excellent General Georg von der Marwitz and they crashed into the southern section of the British line and quickly caused a collapse of resistance there that won back most of the territory lost and more besides. The northern arm of the counterstroke had been halted, so there was no prospect of a greater tactical success and, in an ominous precursor to many such incidents in 1918, Ludendorff noted that the German attack had been frustrated at one stage by a perfectly good division halting its forward movement when it fell upon a well-stocked British supply dump and proceeded to loot it thoroughly.

These remarkable battlefield successes in 1917 were crowned by the complete collapse of one of Germany's principal adversaries. On

7 November the Bolshevik faction led by Vladimir Lenin staged an armed *coup d'état* in Petrograd that overthrew the Russian government and declared its intention to establish a socialist state. It immediately published a decree to the army and the people promising 'peace, land and bread' to a war-weary nation. Within days the revolution had succeeded in seizing control of Petrograd and Moscow and, despite the outbreak of civil war in many places, began to consolidate its 'soviet power'. The cessation of war-fighting on the Eastern Front was an opportunity for Germany to begin the serious transfer of formations from East to West, to carry out the great war-winning stroke that was being considered for 1918.

Things remained uncertain in the East for some time and Ludendorff hints in his memoirs that this uncertainty was ultimately fatal to Germany's ambitions:

> From the end of November onwards troop-trains were incessantly passing from East to West. It was no longer a case of replacing tired divisions in the West by fresh ones, but of really adding to the number of combatants in the West. The training of the troops in the East for western conditions was pushed on, and the same was done in Romania.
>
> The idea of making an attack in France in 1918 attracted many of our generals as early as November, myself perhaps most of all. I therefore eagerly awaited the day when the Russian Government would ask for an armistice. At the front numerous local truces were made in November. Larger and larger formations made overtures to us and already individual Russian Armies made proposals for ceasing hostilities. Peace negotiations were attempted at Dvinsk, but came to nothing. In some places armistices were denounced. It was a confusing picture, half peace, half war.[16]

Perhaps he did not want to be reminded of the irony of the date and place but Ludendorff did not refer specifically to the important conference held at Mons in Belgium on 11 November 1917. Exactly one year before the war was to end, at a place captured by British and Canadian troops within hours of the final armistice, Ludendorff hosted a gathering of the chiefs of staff of the German armies in the West to discuss the ideas advanced by Major Wetzell back in October for a 1918 spring offensive to settle the war in the West once and for all. The prospect of reinforcement from the East was an obvious boost but there was also the sense that Germany had just one last chance to end the war successfully before the strain of going on proved too much.

While keeping an anxious eye on the turbulent East, and coping with the fighting at Cambrai, Ludendorff still had to survey the steep decline in conditions on the German home front. There were desperate food shortages; fodder for draught animals was almost non-existent; coal was scarce, if not as bad as the previous winter; oil reserves were very low. Shortages of textiles, especially cotton, saw the wounded being treated with disgustingly inferior cellulose paper bandages, and the general shortage of paper saw a special army order directing staff officers to write shorter reports with narrower margins, using both sides of the page to write on and reducing the number of copies to the minimum. Better still use the telephone! How long could such emergency measures keep up with the demands of modern industrialised warfare?

The acquisition of Romania was supposed to relieve many of these shortages but so much of her resources were used up keeping armies in the field in the East, and especially to prop up Germany's ailing allies, that there seemed very little left to help Germany. The spirit of the nation seemed at an all time low; revolutionary ideas were spreading through the fleet; party strife was back in the Reichstag. The quality of the troops training in Germany was alarmingly poor. The conscript class of 1919 was already called up and many had died in the later fighting around Passchendaele. The Auxiliary Labour Law as an attempt to mobilise the whole nation behind the war effort had been an abject failure. Using the great prestige of his name, Hindenburg appealed directly to leaders of 'free' trade unions, Christian unions and employee's associations to rally in support of the army and the nation. He invited them to lunch, passed their concerns about labour conditions on to the relevant government agencies and generally tried to impress upon them that he saw himself not as simply the leader of the German armed forces but of the whole nation in arms. Ludendorff recoiled with horror at the suggestion by some ultra-right political figures that he personally should become chancellor and end the fiction that army and government were separate entities.

Germany's allies remained a problem. Austria-Hungary was a spent force but still managed to exasperate her principal backer with endless demands for more material help and with raising diplomatic objections to any German proposals for settling matters in the East. Mesopotamia was lost completely. In Palestine, Turkish troops finally collapsed before the British offensive and the Entente powers were heartened by the 'Christmas gift' of the liberation of Jerusalem. The timely arrival of German troops under Falkenhayn stabilised the front for the winter.

The year ended with armistices in place in Russia and Romania. It had been a remarkable year of military success, of hard won defensive battles in the West and the collapse of major enemy powers in the East and Italy. Everything was to be gathered for one last great effort to force the Entente powers to the peace table from a position of strength in 1918.

*chapter seven*

# The Running Sore in the East

A theme running through the later sections of Ludendorff's memoirs is that the unresolved situation in the East was ultimately fatal to Germany's wartime ambitions. She was not able to transfer enough troops to the West to make a decisive difference there; a million troops were drawn into the endless expanses of Russia and the Ukraine; the insidious influence of communist propaganda worked its way into the German armed forces and society. The collapse of the Tsarist Empire should have been a great blessing; it became a new source of trouble between the Kaiser and the German government and its military leaders.

The new Russian government offered a general armistice towards the end of November 1917 and formal talks began at Brest-Litovsk on 2 December. The details of an armistice were worked out, to be in place until 14 January 1918 but to continue automatically until revoked by either side with seven days notice. Secretary of State Kuhlmann was the principal negotiator for Germany, with General Hoffmann as the Special Representative of General Headquarters; Count Czernin spoke for Austria-Hungary. The latter was quite desperate for peace at any price and would settle for no annexations or claims for compensation. It was he who promoted the idea of turning the meetings into a general

peace conference by inviting all the Entente powers to the talks. The
Bolsheviks treated the whole thing as an enormous exercise in spreading revolutionary propaganda. Backed by the rapacious Turks and
Bulgarians, Germany's military leaders made the most sweeping
demands. Ludendorff briefed Hoffmann to hold out for the Russian
evacuation of Finland, Estonia, Livonia, Bessarabia, Eastern Galicia
and Armenia; for the German annexation of Lithuania, Courland, Riga
and the Baltic islands; for Poland to be 'associated' with Germany; for
compensation to German prisoners of war and for a strong German
role in the Russian economy. At Christmas 1917 Kuhlmann, speaking for
the Foreign Office and the German government, toned these extreme
demands down and insisted that the border states be allowed to vote on
their own future (while under German 'military protection' and led by
blatantly pro-German 'authorities'). The German High Command
totally misunderstood this crafty stand by Kuhlmann and he became
the new traitorous enemy for the German right. The demands of the
military towards their own political institutions reached new heights of
improper arrogance.

Hindenburg felt the army was being betrayed by a government con-
templating a 'peace of reconciliation'. He wrote a long memorandum
to the chancellor expressing his dissatisfaction with the talks:

> For the future course of the proceedings I must therefore have a greater
> influence and the definite right to approve all suggestions and deci-
> sions. In order to judge in each particular case all the consequences
> of any suggestions and decisions I will ask General Hoffmann to send
> me the wording by telegram, and not just by telephone, so that I can
> make my position known.[1]

He went on to say that he could not allow his representative to sign
a 'weak peace'. He was so firmly convinced in his own mind that the
discussions at Brest-Litovsk were primarily about purely military
matters, that he seems to have forgotten that it was the role of the

German civilian government to determine national foreign policy and to sign treaties on behalf of Germany.

While Kuhlmann was attracting party leaders in the Reichstag to his position, Ludendorff was briefing the House Committee of Foreign Affairs that Russia was a beaten enemy, that victory in the West would follow soon, that Germany no longer needed to consider the sensibilities of her own allies or neutral countries and that she needed to make certain military demands in the East as a preparation for the next (inevitable) war with Russia. This was on 2 January 1918, when one of the regular Crown Council meetings was to take place. Before the meeting the Kaiser got into conversation with General Hoffmann and the question of the Polish frontier came up. Hoffmann remarked that Germany actually required very little in the way of annexation to secure a defensible border and the last thing she needed was a great swathe of territory and some two million new Polish citizens. To his lasting dismay the Kaiser seized upon these ideas with enthusiasm and proceeded to present them at the council meeting as his own. Hindenburg and Ludendorff were furious at this 'interference' in a purely military matter. They openly insulted the Kaiser; Ludendorff slammed the door when he stormed out of the room. Both felt betrayed by Hoffmann and, although Ludendorff claimed that it was a temporary rift, their once close relationship was decidedly at an end. It is not certain that they ever spoke directly to each other again.

Ludendorff offered to resign, saying that he was forced to do so by the lack of confidence in him shown by the Kaiser. The right-wing press stormed against Hoffmann and his 'semitic' wife and her parliamentary tea parties. A special army order was published forbidding officers to attend 'political tea parties'. The Crown Prince was drawn in on the side of OHL by his friend Colonel Bauer; Crown Prince Rupert of Bavaria privately expressed his revulsion at this political meddling by German generals. Hindenburg told the Kaiser in a letter dated 7 January 1918 that the army was being ignored by the government on almost every issue. The Hoffmann incident was 'a sign that Your Majesty disregards our judgement on a question which affects the life of the German Fatherland'. In a reasoned and reasonable-sounding plea for understanding he went on:

> It is Your Majesty's exalted right to decide. But Your Majesty will not demand that upright men, who have faithfully served Your Majesty and the country, should lend their authority and their name to acts which, they are profoundly convinced, are dangerous to the Crown and Empire.
>
> Your Majesty will not expect me to submit proposals for operations which are among the most difficult in history unless they are necessary for the attainment of definite military-political goals.
>
> Most humbly I beg Your Majesty to decide on the fundamental principle. Personal considerations regarding General Ludendorff and myself cannot be allowed to count in matters touching the needs of the State.[2]

Both Hindenburg and Ludendorff were now threatening to resign unless Kuhlmann was dismissed. Both also railed against Valentini, the chief of the Kaiser's civil cabinet, whom they blamed for the loss of support in the Reichstag for the army's position. Admiral Müller recorded in his diary (16 January 1918):

> Hindenburg, in a private audience with His Majesty, had said that he could no longer tolerate Valentini as Cabinet Chief. He was entirely to blame for the swing to the Left in the government. The whole army had lost confidence in the Government and the fate of the whole offensive now lay in the balance. More blackmail then! His Majesty was beside himself with rage and treated Hindenburg very roughly, slamming the door and saying: 'I don't need your paternal advice'. Valentini resigned anyway to spare the Kaiser any awkward predicament.[3]

Valentini was replaced by the arch-reactionary Berg, whom Müller described as 'an effective representative of the H-L company'. The German Crown Prince awoke somewhat belatedly to the dangers posed to the House of Hohenzollern by these generals who insisted that they hated involvement in politics. Addressing them both he wrote, 'You cannot demand of my father that he dismisses a statesman every five minutes just because you don't like him'.[4]

Meanwhile, at Brest-Litovsk, the talks dragged on. The Entente powers had, of course, ignored the offer to join the discussions, to the relief of OHL. Hindenburg instructed Hoffmann to step up the pressure for a settlement as the demands of the great Western offensive required an end to the uncertainty in the East. A wave of overtly political strikes in Berlin at the end of January had alarmed OHL and the last straw came when Bolshevik agitators appealed over the radio directly to German troops to refuse obedience to the Kaiser.

As the Baltic states came under increasing pressure from Communist insurgents, and Finland stood on the brink of civil war, Hoffmann presented Leon Trotsky with an ultimatum to sign a peace treaty or face renewed military action. Trotsky rejected the peace demand and instead announced the complete demobilisation of the Russian Army. This presented the German authorities with a potential for chaos in the East and the military leaders moved swiftly to intervene decisively. At a meeting on 13 February 1918 the civilian leaders tried to dissuade the soldiers from renewed action, insisting that it would not be popular in the country. Hindenburg forcefully persuaded them that it was necessary to protect German minorities in Latvia and Estonia, to offer help to Germany's new allies in Finland and the Ukraine and, most of all, to end the war in the East and free up troops for the Western offensives.

On 16 February the Russian government was told that the armistice was over and that German 'police actions' would be necessary. On 18 February fifty-two German divisions under Field Marshal Eichhorn, with General Groener as his chief of staff, attacked eastwards, against a collapsing Russian Army. It was a march of triumph. These mainly Landwehr divisions swept over Russia and the Ukraine as far as Orsha, Mogilev and Rostov. By 25 February the Soviets declared they would sign any treaty put before them. The Treaty of Brest-Litovsk was signed by 3 March. In it Russia lost 90 per cent of her coal, 54 per cent of her industry, 34 per cent of her population, 33 per cent of her railways, 32 per cent of her agricultural land and all her oil and cotton production. While Germany went wild with joy, the peoples of the rest of the world saw what peace with Germany was really like and drew their own conclusions. Ludendorff insisted that Germany had shown a 'lamb-like patience' with the Bolshevik regime and resented this being called a 'peace of violence'. A similarly harsh peace treaty was forced upon Romania later in 1918.

Now Germany found herself occupying the vast empty reaches of Russia and the Ukraine. Large numbers of troops were swallowed up in garrison duties and in a number of economic tasks. There was renewed fighting in the Ukraine as Red forces attacked the regime sympathetic to Germany. Far from providing wealth and supplies to a beleaguered Germany, the East was swallowing up resources. Catastrophic harvest failures meant the army of occupation could barely feed itself. Germany had to export 80,000 tons of coal to get the Ukraine's railways back in action. Coal production in the East totalled a poor five million tons (down from fifteen million tons in a strike-torn 1917). When Germany created two divisions from Ukrainian prisoners of war and sent them east to serve their new country, they disintegrated under a blizzard of Red propaganda within two weeks.

Against the advice of the political leaders who could see another drain on Germany's shrinking resources opening up, German troops were also dispatched to Finland to help Mannerheim's 'white' forces chase out the 'reds'. As late as August 1918, when the Western Front was about to collapse under Entente attacks, Ludendorff was personally embroiled in talks with the Soviet government about lending German troops to help expel Entente forces from those parts of Russia under attack from them. Since he would only agree if Germany could occupy Petrograd, Lenin soon lost interest in the idea. In September, with the Western Front under even greater pressure, Ludendorff was involved in discussions about a future king of Finland.

When Germany embraced the cause of anti-communist forces in Georgia it brought her to a critical stand-off with her Turkish ally. The lure of an Eastern empire seems a never-ending distraction to the OHL leaders. Dreams of creating German colonies in the Crimea one moment, disposing of the Russian Black Sea to their allies, without consulting German naval opinion, the next. Hindenburg and Ludendorff even turned on Admiral Holtzendorff when he objected to their interference in an obviously naval matter and forced his resignation. The old admiral's complaints to the Kaiser about their 'megalomania' came too late to save him.

Even at the height of the crisis in the West in the autumn of 1918, Germany was too heavily engaged in the East to release troops in any significant numbers for service there. There was more than a hint that the Eastern troops were so heavily infected with socialist ideas by then that they would constitute an even greater danger to the Fatherland.

*chapter eight*

# Victory Must Be Ours

OHL had calculated that they would have a numerical advantage over the
Entente powers on the Western Front for the whole of spring 1918 and
for most of the summer and into the autumn. This was the 'window of
opportunity' to which they bent all their plans for that year. By the end
of November 1917 the number of German divisions on the Western
Front rose from 150 to 160 and the total rose to 171 by the end of the
year. By February 1918 it was 180 and on the eve of the great offensive
it peaked at 193 divisions and three independent brigades. Three and
a half million men stood in the West for the last bid for victory. With
fifty-three divisions and thirteen brigades (one million men) in the East,
and only one division each in the Balkans, Turkey and at home, it can be
seen that three-quarters of the German field army had been concentrated there. Ludendorff would have liked to add allied divisions to his
order of battle, especially the Turkish XV Corps, but the situation was
so dire in other theatres that he had to be content to see them release
German divisions for service in the West.

In discussions with Naval High Command it was accepted that the
submarine campaign of 1917 had failed in the large economic objectives it had set itself. OHL allowed that the submarines could continue
to make an important contribution to the overall strategy and agreed

to divert industrial resources to the construction programme needed to keep up the pressure. At the very least it was hoped that the sinking of enemy shipping would delay the deployment of the American Army to Europe. The Germans were clearly beginning to worry about the large numbers of American troops that would eventually be sent to France but they were certain that they could never compensate for the total loss of the Russian armies to the Entente, and that they would arrive too late to influence the course of the German offensives of 1918.

The German defensive victories of 1917 had been won at a terrible cost. The material weight of the enemy attacks had been hard to bear and the defenders were steadily beaten back despite the strength of their positions and the losses they inflicted on the attackers. Their fear was that 1918 would see more of such crushing attacks, better co-ordinated and over wider fronts. The army in the West was becoming a brittle instrument. There were shamefully high numbers of 'skulkers', not outright deserters but men who evaded their duty whenever things got too hot. The real fighting fell on relatively few front fighters and their fighting spirit was worn down by years of defensive battle. The army pined for the offensive according to OHL planners.

At the Mons conference on 11 November 1917 the chiefs of staff of the Western armies met with the operations section of the OHL to discuss the possibilities for offensive action in 1918. The main army groups had their own ideas for the principal lines of operation. For the Crown Prince of Bavaria's army group, General Hermann von Kuhl suggested the attack be directed against the vital railway junction of Hazebrouck, the loss of which would ruin the lines of communication of the entire British sector on the Western Front and, by threatening the Channel ports, put their very existence on the Continent in jeopardy. For the Crown Prince of Prussia, General Friederich von der Schulen-burg proposed an attack either side of Verdun to defeat the French first and then turn against the British. A third possibility was to strike at the junction of the French and British armies along the axis St

Quentin–Amiens. These broad avenues of approach were the same ones discussed at every stage of the war by OHL from the closing days of 1914 onwards. In 1915 Colonel Seeckt, at the behest of Falkenhayn, had drawn up a scheme that bore a remarkable similarity to the final 1918 plan, before he was sent to the East for the battle of Gorlice-Tarnow.

It was the success at Caporetto and the hasty dispatch of British and French divisions to Italy that suggested that the balance of forces on the Western Front might tilt in Germany's favour for just long enough for a decision to be obtained there. Hence the memorandum by Major Wetzell of 23 October 1917 calling for a spring offensive. The Mons conference was already planned when the Bolsheviks seized power and effectively took Russia out of the war. The possibilities suddenly took on new dimensions, but they were still just ideas being debated. Nothing could be firmly undertaken until the situation in the East was clearly settled.

Ludendorff guided the discussions at Mons. To Kuhl he replied that the ground in Flanders remained too wet for active operations until April. It would be necessary to attack well before then, in late February or early March, in order to anticipate any enemy offensive. In particular he wanted to forestall another punishing British offensive in Flanders. The steady arrival of American reinforcements was another factor making an early start a preferred option. To Schulenburg he replied that the French had shown an alarming recovery from their low point in 1917, that they would fight stubbornly at Verdun, and that the British would come to their assistance by launching the very offensive he most feared. Germany would be facing two major battles at once and would again be responding to Western Allied initiatives in one of them. He summarised his arguments under three headings – that the uncertain situation in the East only released about thirty-five divisions and a thousand guns for one powerful blow in the West; that this blow should be delivered as early as possible before the Americans became a factor; and that he recognised his country's most implacable enemy with the simple statement: 'We must beat the British'. The strength of the British was massed in the northern sectors of the front, guarding their vital lifelines through the Channel ports. It might be more fruitful to attack further to the south: 'In particular an attack near St Quentin appeared promising. After gaining the Somme line, Ham–Peronne, operations could be carried further in a north-westerly direction, with the left flank resting on the Somme, and lead to the rolling up of the British front'.[1] This was the genesis of Operation Michael but nothing was decided at this meeting and the debate between some of the greatest planning minds of the German army went on for many weeks.

On 20 November 1917 Kuhl sent a long memorandum to Ludendorff expanding his thoughts on the various schemes proposed. He was anxious to avoid another British offensive because he knew that 'defensive battles, from long experience, brought more losses than the attack'. He still favoured a strike against the British in the Estaires-Armentières area because of the important and immediate strategic results of a breakthrough there. He had already singled out the sector held by the Portuguese as a weak point to aim for. The Arras area was too heavily defended to be attacked profitably. St Quentin could certainly be attacked at any time and was relatively weakly held; the junction between two armies (the British and the French) was always a vulnerable point. But he did warn at this early stage that the Germans would then have to cross the very area they had so thoroughly devastated in the 1917 retreat, and would have to make awkward changes in the main directions of the attack as the battle unfolded. In December he made the further observation that the British seemed greatly weakened by their losses in late 1917 and might not be able to attack at an early date in 1918. This made operations in Flanders in April even more attractive.

On 12 December Lieutenant Colonel Wetzell introduced the idea of a series of offensives. He knew that true surprise was extremely difficult to obtain in modern mass warfare. At best the German armies could hope for a 'good start' over their enemy and then let the speed of operations determine later moves. Personally he still favoured an attack at

Verdun but he could see the strategic advantages of a success against the British at Hazebrouck. He proposed a sequence of attacks, beginning with one at St Quentin to draw British reserves down from the north, followed after a couple of weeks by the main blow in Flanders. The British official historian commented dryly, 'Fortunately for us, Lieutenant Colonel Wetzell's proposals were not accepted'. When the Germans did launch the Flanders attack it was 'too late'.

A major conference on 27 December 1917 set the final planning in motion. Crown Prince Rupert's army group was directed to prepare for attacks at Armentières (Operation George), Ypres (George II), Arras (Mars), and St Quentin (Michael). Various other smaller operations along the Western Front were to be worked out and all was to be ready by 10 March 1918. A new Eighteenth Army, under the command of the redoubtable Hutier, was inserted into the line, on the left of Marwitz's Second Army and Below's Seventeenth Army. These generals were all masters of the new offensive doctrine. After a tour of the Western Front armies, in the company of Kuhl and Schulenburg, Ludendorff announced his final decision on 21 January 1918. Operation George was too dependent on the vagaries of Flanders weather and Operation Mars faced too powerful a defensive system. Operation Michael would be carried out between the Oise and the Scarpe.

Michael was scheduled for 20 March, with Bapaume, Peronne and Ham as its general objectives, as preparation for the vital Mars attack on Arras several days later. This was the blow that would completely unhinge the British lines and allow them to be rolled up from south to north and trap the BEF against the Channel coast. Planning meetings took place in February that incorporated alternative attacks if any of the first were brought to a stop. Ludendorff was quite prepared to begin operations against the French while the main battle was in progress against the British. The several variants of Operation George against the British in Flanders were to be ready for April, dependent on the release of the 'battering train' of heavy artillery, trench mortar and

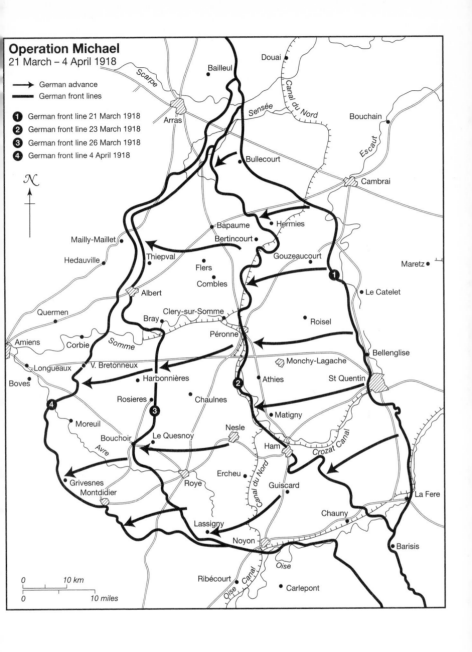

**Operation Michael**
21 March – 4 April 1918

→ German advance
━━ German front lines

**1** German front line 21 March 1918
**2** German front line 23 March 1918
**3** German front line 26 March 1918
**4** German front line 4 April 1918

N

Scarpe

Bailleul

Douai

Canal du Nord

Sensée

Bouchain

Arras

Bullecourt

Cambrai

Escaut

Bapaume

Hermies

Bertincourt

Gouzeaucourt

Maretz

Mailly-Maillet

Thiepval

Flers

**1**

Le Catelet

Hedauville

Combles

Albert

Clery-sur-Somme

Bray

Péronne

Roisel

Quermen

Somme

Monchy-Lagache

Bellenglise

Amiens

Corbie

V. Bretonneux

Athies

St Quentin

Longueaux

Boves

Harbonnières

**2**

Rosieres

Chaulnes

Matigny

**4**

**3**

Moreuil

Le Quesnoy

Nesle

Bouchoir

Ham

Crozat Canal

Avre

Ercheu

Canal du Nord

Guiscard

La Fere

Grivesnes

Roye

Montdidier

Chauny

Lassigny

Noyon

Barisis

Oise

Ribécourt

Oise Canal

Carlepont

0 ——— 10 km
0 ——— 10 miles

aircraft assets for redeployment to the north. Diversionary efforts all along the line as far as Belfort were also prepared. The original plan was to let Eighteenth Army form a flank guard along the Crozat Canal–River Somme line while the Seventeenth and Second armies carried out the main attacks. Early in 1918 the German planners noted that the British were taking over a large section of front from the French, down to the Oise Valley. Now the Germans would not strike the junction between the Allies but would hit the British at all points. As this was their principal adversary, this pleased them. It was also thought that the French would not be in a great hurry to come to the aid of their allies until they were sure that their own front was not in danger of attack.

The planners dealing with the Eighteenth Army's role soon began to argue for an increased level of activity. A passive defence of the southern edge of the battle area would tie down large numbers of troops unproductively. On 3 March Ludendorff agreed to the idea that they should push out beyond the canal–river line and fight their enemies in the open wherever they found them. When requests started to be made upon the Seventh Army to release divisions to assist this move, the Crown Prince of Prussia made his bid for an enhanced role in the offensive. Before long the Eighteenth Army was transferred to his army group and, with the Seventh Army, was to play a major part in the attack, but the principal effort was to be against the British towards the north. The final orders for the attack on 21 March went out under Hindenburg's signature on 10 March 1918.

Just as winter 1916–17 had been devoted to a major revision of defence doctrine, so the winter of 1917–18 was spent teaching new attack methods to the German field army. *The Offensive Battle in Position Warfare* was a multi-volume manual covering every aspect of the attack. All the excellent offensive principles of the pre-war regulations were to be revived and adapted to the new conditions. Ludendorff stressed that they needed to restore open manoeuvre warfare but without the shocking level of casualties sustained in 1914. It would not be easy to end the defensive mentality and restore the attacking spirit. Concentrating overwhelming force against weak points of opposition would ensure the breakthrough; seizing the high ground assumed its old great tactical importance. The preservation of scarce manpower was desperately important; the battle was to be fought principally with the machinery of war, not with profligate use of soldiers' bodies. Fighting lines were to be kept thin and constantly fed with reinforcements from the rear. Mass tactics were to be avoided.

The light machine-gun was now considered the principal infantry weapon, supported by riflemen, and this basic infantry group had its firepower enhanced by the addition of quick-firing and high-trajectory weapons. Heavy machine-guns and light trench mortars were vital as close support weapons in the attack. Within the divisions field guns were deployed forward to battalions and regiments as 'infantry guns'. Medium trench mortars and flamethrowers were assigned to divisions. There would be great support from the air force, both in a direct combat air-to-ground role, as well as the usual struggle for air supremacy and spotting for the guns. The artillery would be decisive and was concentrated in unprecedented numbers and given fire missions of the greatest weight and intensity. The expenditure of ammunition was almost beyond comprehension. The art of camouflage reached new heights as the guns and ammunition were moved up to the front in secrecy.

A huge programme of training was set in course, behind the Western Front itself but also in Russia and Romania. Officers skilled in Western Front fighting went out to the Eastern divisions selected for the offensive to teach the new techniques. An intensive three-week course of training at the divisional level was designed to make sure all the components of the division functioned properly. A total of fifty-six divisions and a large proportion of the artillery went through this special course. These divisions received the most and the best in the way of new equipment. Their draught animals received greatly enhanced supplies of fodder. Many other divisions received the new manuals and carried out their own training. Other divisions were nominated as 'position' divisions and knew they would not be used in an offensive role. Generals and their staffs also went through intensive training in handling their units at the new high tempo of operations. Special courses for junior officers, down to the level of 'group' leaders, were organised; all attack troops underwent training using live ammunition. Ludendorff reported a lively interest and discussion of the new attack doctrine and he was confident of its ultimate success.

The old way of setting objective lines to be achieved by a certain time was done away with. Now the attack was to break in to the enemy position, up to the line of his field artillery, and then to breakthrough and exploit the battle as it developed naturally. Attacking units were to press forward regardless of the situation on their flanks; strong points of resistance were to be bypassed and dealt with by stronger follow-on units. Specially trained and heavily armed storm troops, at anything up to battalion strength, were to lead the attacks, probing for weak points to infiltrate the enemy position to its whole depth. Reserves would be fed in to exploit every success and the whole battle would be allowed to unfold as the situation demanded. This was designed to confound the enemy and keep them in a state of constant dissolution. The artillery programme would create the conditions for the initial breakthrough, and would endeavour to support the infantry in its forward movement by responding to light signals. The nature of the battle would deny the use of the more traditional 'creeping barrage' after the first assault. To anyone familiar with British infantry attack methods in 1917 and 1918 it seems curious that Ludendorff spends a good deal of time in his memoirs extolling the virtues of the creeping barrage, and the need for the infantry to keep very close to it, even to the extent of taking casualties from their own artillery rather than from an unsuppressed machine-gun nest, as if this was some new revelation for 1918. Of more importance were the new instructions for how the infantry was to conduct itself once it had pushed beyond the effective range of protective barrages. It would be vulnerable while batteries were moved up to support it, and they would never regain the power of the opening attack. Hence the call for pushing the attack to the absolute limit and being prepared to revert to the defensive when resistance stiffened as it inevitably would. At that stage the offensive would be resumed on another sector, putting greater and greater strain on the whole enemy front.

While Ludendorff sensed that the morale of the Western armies was improved by the prospect of ending trench deadlock and forcing their enemies to the peace table, he was also aware of dangerous forces at work sapping the will of the German people to continue the struggle. It was already known that 10 per cent of the troops being moved from the East to the West had jumped from the trains and deserted. The Germans had a long standing habit of saying that this increased the reliability and efficiency of the remaining troops,[2] but Ludendorff continued to worry about the influence of socialist revolutionaries in the army. In a frankly honest appraisal he likened the armies of 1918 to 'a kind of militia with much experience of war' when compared to the armies of 1914. He thought that the enemy was no better and that, if mobile warfare was restored, the German soldier would adapt to it very much better than his adversaries.

Professional soldiers knew that every great enterprise in war was fraught with uncertainty and danger. At an audience with the Kaiser on 13 February, when Hindenburg and Ludendorff had to go through the formality of obtaining the supreme warlord's sanction for the offensive, Ludendorff addressed his kaiser and the imperial chancellor in the following way:

> The battle in the West is the greatest task that has ever been imposed upon an army, and one which England and France have been trying for two years to compass. Yesterday I spoke with the Commander of the Seventh Army; he told me that the more he thought about this task, the more impressed he was with its magnitude. That is how all

responsible men in the West should think. I believe, too, that I, who have to furnish the Field-Marshal with the foundation on which he bases his request for His Majesty's decision, am more than anyone impressed with the immensity of the undertaking. It can only be successfully accomplished if the authorities who conduct the war are relieved of all intolerable shackles, if the very last man is employed in the decisive conflict, and is animated, not only by love for his Emperor and his native land, but by confidence in the strength of the military leadership and the greatness of our country. These spiritual forces cannot be underestimated, they are the foundation of the greatest deeds. They must be strengthened by the energy of our action in the East. The Army in the West is waiting for the opportunity to act.

We must not imagine that this offensive will be like those in Galicia or Italy; it will be an immense struggle that will begin at one point, continue at another, and take a long time; it is difficult, but it will be victorious ...[3]

On the front chosen for the first assaults a great preponderance of the attacking forces was concentrated. Behind the eleven divisions holding the front lines of the Eighteenth, Second and Seventeenth armies there were aligned sixty assault divisions in three waves, with another three OHL reserve divisions to hand. Thus a total of seventy-four divisions faced the thirty divisions of the British Fifth and Third armies in the area to be attacked. The attack was supported by 950 field batteries, 701 heavy batteries and 55 super-heavy batteries (a total of 6,473 guns and howitzers), 3,532 trench mortars, 77 flights of aircraft and 5 bombing squadrons. All ammunition dumps were in place by 15 March. All extra guns and mortars were moved up between 11 and 19 March and were emplaced by 20 March. The sixty assault divisions began their approach march on the 16th, were rested on the night of 18–19 March and were in place by 20 March. Increased activity along almost the whole length of the Western Front was designed to mask the real frontage of the attack.

Crown Prince Rupert of Bavaria had a healthy respect for the British enemy he had fought for so long. He was fully aware of their stubborn character and had few illusions about the difficulty of the task. Ludendorff himself was quite aware of the nature of the gamble. He repeated the mantra that 'strategy is made up of expedients' and that 'strategic victory follows tactical success'. To the persistent questioning of Rupert about the goal of the offensive, he retorted: 'We make a hole and the rest will take care of itself'. This must have been based on an expectation that the German Army could respond rapidly to sudden changes in the general strategic situation as it developed following immediate battlefield successes. It was how things had been done in Russia so well for so long. It expected a great deal of an army largely dependent on emaciated horses and mules for its mobility, for its 35,000 trucks, with their inefficient iron wheels, could not be relied on to keep up a rapid momentum of operations alone.

OHL moved up to Spa and an advanced headquarters opened at Avesnes in France. It had been the habit of some General Staff officers to consult the semi-occult writings of the Moravian Brethren on the eve of great events. The text for 21 March was, 'This is the day of the chosen people'. Inspired by the message, Hindenburg and Ludendorff unleashed their massed armies on the expectant British and French.

The Western Allies were expecting a German offensive and were in the process of reorganising and improving their defences to meet it. This enormous task came at the same time as the British, facing something of a manpower crisis, were reducing their infantry divisions from twelve to nine battalions, while simultaneously doubling the number of Lewis light machine-guns per battalion. Despite these enormous distractions, they faced the enemy with confidence, fully expecting to punish the German attackers in much the same way as they had themselves been handled in their major attacks of the two previous years. What they could not have predicted was the awesome power of the opening bombardment organised by Colonel Bruchmüller for 21 March.

Through many battles in his two years on the Eastern Front this quiet, studious officer of the heavy artillery, called out of retirement in 1914, had developed his technique of centralised control of the entire artillery assets of the attack formations he was associated with. (He never commanded more than a divisional artillery; he was an 'artillery adviser' employed wherever he was needed.) He drew up the most intricate bombardment plans to deliver the maximum concentration of fire over the whole depth of the positions to be attacked in as short a space of time and as violent a manner as possible.

At 04.40 hours along a forty-four mile front the greatest weight of artillery fire ever seen hit the positions of the British Third and Fifth armies. For two hours the target was the British artillery emplacements and command and control centres. A special feature of Bruchmüller's tactics was the very high proportion of gas used, as much as four gas shells to every one of high explosive. This incapacitated the enemy without doing so much damage to the ground as to impede movement. The various elements of the heavy and field artillery and the trench mortars then followed a complex programme for the next two hours of bringing fire to bear on the British front and support lines, while the rear areas were constantly under attack of some sort. The weight of fire waxed and waned and shifted back and forth and ended with five minutes of incredible intensity on the front-line trench. At 09.40 hours the creeping barrage heralded the advance of the German infantry, who were greatly assisted by the fog that blanketed most of the battlefield.

Over most of the front the dazed defenders of the forward zone were overwhelmed quickly. They were not able to perform their function of disorganising the attack before it reached the battle zone. The fighting in the battle zone itself varied in nature from place to place. Where the leading attackers were able to infiltrate between strong points and uncover the flanks of the defenders they caused major retreats. Elsewhere, where the artillery had perhaps been not so effective or, as was often the case, where the fog cleared more quickly, the stubborn defenders inflicted very severe losses on the attackers. At the end of the first day the Germans had made important inroads into the British positions but had suffered heavy losses of some of their best troops. Over the next few days the most successful German units forced a general retreat upon the whole British line which soon found itself back behind the Somme, losing in a couple of days all the ground they had spent four and a half months fighting for in 1916. With an impressive capture of prisoners and guns, and a spectacular gain of ground the Germans had certainly restored a 'war of movement' to the Western Front, and the movement was all in their favour.

But there was a fatal flaw in their progress and it comes out in the subdued manner that Ludendorff describes the campaign in his memoirs. He highlights the problems faced by the Seventeenth Army as it faced the much stronger defences of the British Third Army and how it suffered heavy losses and delays while the Second and Eighteenth armies made much better progress to the south. In fact the Eighteenth Army made spectacular advances towards the south-west and drove a significant gap between the British and the French which caused a real crisis between the Allies as the French were reluctant to move to help the British until they were quite certain that no major attack was going to fall on their lines. Ludendorff relates that, as the resistance to the north was hardening and progress was impeded by the old Somme crater fields, the original idea was modified and the major rail centre of Amiens was the new focus of the offensive. He played down the ill-fated attack, Operation Mars, on 28 March. This was to be the decisive blow at Arras that was to break the BEF and drive in behind it and start a retreat all the way to the Channel ports. The attack was defeated so completely and comprehensively that it was referred to as Germany's 1st of July (a reference to the British disaster on the first day of the battle of the Somme in 1916). He simply stated that the Seventeenth Army 'fought under an unlucky star', which hardly rates as a useful analysis. Ludendorff gives sparse details as he explains that the fighting around Amiens turned into exactly that 'battle of exhaustion' that Germany could not afford, and that he closed down the indecisive operation in order to renew the pressure elsewhere.

He took some comfort in the brilliant feats of the German troops and the way they had broken through strong defences and rapidly gained large tracts of enemy territory: 'Our troops had beaten the French and English and proved themselves superior'. However he refused to accept that the basic concept of the offensives was at fault and instead criticised his troops:

> Generally speaking, our tactics had proved sound. What had happened in the Seventeenth Army did not necessitate any fundamental changes, although some lessons needed more drastic application. Above all, the infantry must be more extended. At many places machine-gun posts had given us an undue amount of trouble and so caused delay. The infantry groups had often been lacking in initiative, and their co-operation with the auxiliary arms had often failed. The troops had found special difficulty in reorganizing them-selves for defence at the conclusion of the attack, and particularly in recognising when no further success was to be gained by continuing the attack. All troops, especially mounted troops, had suffered heavily from bombing by hostile airmen.[4]

He said that the troops were not always under the firm control of their officers and referred specifically to the problem of them falling upon the huge Allied store dumps and looting them and the disruption of the advance that this caused. Having been reliably informed that the Allies were starving because of the brilliant submarine blockade, it was a blow to German morale when they found so much good food and drink abandoned in such quantities.

The first stage of the 'peace offensives' had left Germany with a great bulging salient to defend, using some very tired divisions who hoped to get a rest in the process. Ludendorff himself had to identify the body of yet another of his pilot officer stepsons. He hoped that the severe blow delivered against the French and British would be reinforced by another delivered along the Lys River in Flanders.

On 9 April the Germans were again aided by fog and by a formidable opening artillery bombardment. Where they struck the front line manned by the wretched Portuguese they tore a great gap through which the attackers poured and unhinged the British line, except at its southern edge where the German attack was totally defeated by the 55th (West Lancashire) Division. For some days the Germans made progress, sufficient to alarm the taciturn Field Marshal Haig enough to issue his famous 'Backs to the Wall' appeal to the British Army in the field. For Ludendorff it was a catalogue of unsatisfactory results from the first day. He complained on 10 April that his troops were more interested in looting Allied supply dumps than in clearing out machine-gun nests. On Haig's day of crisis, 12 April, Ludendorff could see the attack momentum falling off. Even if the attacks were pressed until the important position of Mount Kemmel was captured on 25 April, the front was stabilised by French reinforcements flooding into the area and the Germans were left with yet another awkward salient to defend.

Ludendorff, after congratulating his troops on achieving another great tactical victory over their enemies, launched a ferocious attack on the lack of discipline of the soldiers, the poor levels of leadership displayed by officers and the general decline of soldierly qualities in the army, singling out the War Ministry for its meddling leniency. In an effort to reduce a perceived widening rift between officers and men, they had abolished certain field punishments available to officers, which Ludendorff lamented. He points out that the training grounds reported a 'tired and discontented spirit which was being brought into the Army from home'. The only 'new' drafts to make up losses were wounded men being sent back to the front. Men returning from leave were found to be heavily influenced by agitators and the generally low level of morale on the home front. Troops coming from the East were a particularly bad influence.

The army had to be prepared for a renewed offensive. The heavy losses amongst officers meant that the Germans would have to leave out of any future attacks a 'battle reserve' of experienced officers to reconstruct their units after the pounding they took in new attacks. The BEF had been doing that for about eighteen months. 'It was necessary to instruct the troops according to the tactical lessons learned in the latest fighting. These were, more extended formations for infantry, greater importance to be attached to storm-troop tactics, better co-operation between groups and companion arms, and between infantry and artillery'. Again these are elementary ideas that had been learnt by the BEF the hard way in nearly two years of attacking German trenches; it reinforces the impression that Ludendorff was imparting some fairly basic ideas in the middle of a great series of battles to an army looking more and more like a kind of militia. The whole of the 28th Division and elements of the 3rd Jager Battalion were designated as 'demonstration units' and served at Avesnes to teach assault tactics to the rest of the army. 'On all occasions I emphasised the need of not forgetting the necessary formation for defence, and of recognising the moment when the attack must be stopped and the defence resumed. This must be felt by the systematic hardening of the enemy's resistance'.[5] Meanwhile each infantry company got a fifth light machine-gun; more anti-aircraft machine guns were issued to transport units; the first anti-tank rifles reached the men in the line. The fodder for the horses improved slightly but, with Germany's allies a continual drain on her food resources, not much could be done to improve rations for the men, which left them in a weakened state when the first signs of the Spanish influenza epidemic began to appear.

By the middle of May the artillery (working to another Bruchmüller plan) and a new wave of attack divisions were in place facing the French along the Chemin des Dames ridge and the Aisne River. The powerful attack launched on 27 May was another stunning success, helped by the intransigence of the local French commander who kept far too many troops in the forward trenches to be destroyed by the bombardment and assault. The German Seventh Army reached the Marne and pushed its right out to Château-Thierry (where it encountered stubborn American forces) and its left out towards Rheims, in conjunction with the First Army. Still Ludendorff bemoaned the fact that the attack had been held up around Soissons and the battle was broken off early in June. Despite another clear-cut tactical victory and a renewed threat to Paris reminiscent of the heady days of 1914, the Germans were rewarded with a barrage of ferocious and defiant proclamations by Georges Clemenceau, living up to his nickname of 'Tiger'. Clearly the Entente powers were not yet ready for peace. When the attack was renewed on 9 June to improve the local situation it had to be broken off after two days under an increasing number of French counter-attacks.

The early dismissal of the effect of the Americans on the overall strategic position was having to be revised somewhat hurriedly. German intelligence had identified twenty American divisions ready for action, and these divisions were twice as large as those of the other combatants on the Western Front. This was more than Ludendorff had believed possible and he later thought that the relief they were able to provide to the battered French and British armies became the deciding factor in the war.

Ludendorff briefly considered going over to the defensive but dismissed the idea because the offensive was ultimately less demanding on the men and incurred no higher losses. Hindenburg and he thought that one more great blow would produce the victory that would force the Entente powers to the peace table. They still wanted to settle accounts with the British in Flanders but the Western Allies were too strong there. A major attack aimed at Rheims would draw in all the French reserves. They had deduced that the increased use of black colonial troops meant the French were on their knees and had no further powers of resistance. Within two weeks of the third great blow the 'battering train' could be moved north and the final offensive of the war carried out.

While the army was being prepared for its last big push the situation on the home front went from bad to worse. Ludendorff gives a litany of events that show the inexorable collapse of the German will to fight: the Prince Lichnowsky pamphlet holding Germany to blame for the war, the high desertion rate amongst Alsatian troops, the secessionist tendencies in Bavaria and denunciations of this 'Prussian' war, and mutinous activity in the Belgian training camps. There was a wave of criticism of the officer corps in general and the staff officers in particular to which Ludendorff took special exception: 'Yet is there not a man who does not know of the nerve-wracking work and colossal burden they bear unceasingly? The troops were relieved, but the staff remained on duty, day and night. For four years I endured this state of tension without rest or relief. In such circumstances I could not live on field-kitchen rations'.[6] As this tide of criticism of the perquisites of an officer's life gained pace Ludendorff did, somewhat sardonically, offer to place OHL on field-kitchen rations if the government ministries did the same. He was not surprised that his offer was not taken up.

It is a sign that the German leadership was beginning to see just how bad things were when Ludendorff suggested to Secretary of State Kuhlmann that peace feelers should be put out immediately, with a conciliatory declaration about the future of Belgium. The foreign secretary thought that this was pointless in the face of Clemenceau's intransigence. Instead he delivered a speech to the Reichstag on 24 June 1918 in which he admitted that the Western Allies saw German peace offers as diplomatic traps and he stated in public for the first time that there was no military solution to this war as far as Germany was concerned. This brought a storm of protest from the nationalist elements of the population and OHL began immediately to agitate for Kuhlmann's dismissal. By early July he had been replaced by a more 'acceptable' candidate.

In a curious passage of his memoirs Ludendorff went to some trouble to defend his last offensive as something other than a forlorn hope: 'The attack on Rheims was based on sound military principles, and we undertook the operation with the firm conviction that it would succeed'. He insisted that the German soldier was still capable of fighting well 'as long as they were handled carefully and with an eye to their peculiarities and temperament'.[7] The attack was carried out by the Crown Prince of Prussia's group of armies, with Colonel Bruchmuller again directing the artillery effort. The Seventh Army would attack west of Rheims; the First and Third armies east of it, with the large objective of uniting on the line Épernay–Châlons, encircling the city and its garrison. This was not a drive on Paris but another effort to draw in the French reserves while leaving Crown Prince Rupert's armies free to rest and prepare for the decisive Flanders offensive that was to follow.

German intelligence was aware from the reports of deserters of large concentrations of French armoured forces near Villers-Cotterêts, but a new Ninth Army had been organised (based on an experienced army headquarters brought in from Romania) and inserted into the line on the right of the Seventh Army to protect its flank. Ludendorff had to admit that he was wholly unaware of just how much the French knew about the impending attack. Apart from the usual difficulty of keeping secret the organisation of a major assault on the Western Front, the French had captured many prisoners who divulged the time and place of the attack, and many details seemed to be common gossip through most of Germany.

The attack went in on 15 July and showed some considerable success on the Seventh Army's front where they struck Italian divisions in the line and penetrated three miles south of the Marne. Progress was much slower on the 16 July. But east of Rheims the French skilfully evacuated their first positions before the bombardment fell, and totally defeated the German attack before their second positions, from where the French artillery delivered crushing fire on the hapless German infantry. It was such a complete failure that OHL cancelled all further attacks on this sector and returned the assault divisions to army group reserves. On

17 July it was decided to abandon the whole effort and pull the Seventh Army back to its start line on the night of 20–21 July.

Artillery and air assets were being withdrawn for the Flanders offensive, and Ludendorff himself went to Crown Prince Rupert's headquarters on 17 July to discuss the attack of the Fourth and Sixth armies towards the vital rail junction of Hazebrouck. It was there that he heard of the crushing assault by the French on 18 July to the south-west of Soissons. The German front was shattered by the mass use of tanks, artillery and infantry. All Crown Prince William's reserves were drawn in to try and heal the breach. Ludendorff immediately released OHL reserves for the same purpose and rushed back by train to Avesnes. Hindenburg met him at the station and informed him of the seriousness of the situation. He reported the success of the huge numbers of French light tanks and the alarming sight of troop-carrying tanks conveying French machine guns and infantry deep into the German positions and returning for further loads with impunity. French artillery could now shell the major railways supporting the German front and reinforcements were obliged to detrain some distance away and in some disorder. The troops south of the Marne were evacuated in haste but with great skill. Using the able General Lossberg as a roving liaison officer, the German commanders soon determined on a major evacuation of the whole Marne salient back to more defensible lines. By the end of July the Flanders offensive was officially cancelled and the whole initiative on the Western Front had shifted inexorably to the Entente powers. The divisions earmarked for the final offensive were rushed south to shore up a sagging front line. Towards the end of July Ludendorff noticed a slackening of the tempo and was grateful for it. He praised the resilience of the German soldier in stabilising the front, poured scorn on American troops and grieved for the weakened and exhausted state of his German infantry divisions. In early August he hoped for a quiet period to rest and replenish his battered armies. All that was about to change forever.

*chapter nine*

# The Road to Defeat

Perhaps the best known quotation of the First World War is Ludendorff's admission: 'August 8th was the black day of the German Army in the history of this war'. His following remarks show that this was the start of a process in which things began to unravel very quickly: 'This was the worst experience that I had to go through, except for the events that, from September 15th onwards, took place on the Bulgarian Front and sealed the fate of the Quadruple Alliance'.[1]

What was it about 8 August that caused Ludendorff so much concern? The German Army had received punishing attacks from the BEF before without this crisis of confidence – 9 April, 7 June, 20 September and 20 November 1917 all spring to mind. The attack was so well executed, and more importantly, so well organised with such a high degree of secrecy, that it must have given warning that the BEF was very far from beaten, despite the defeats inflicted upon it in March and April. The presence of the Canadian Corps had been concealed by a masterful use of signals intelligence and disinformation. A fine co-ordination of British, Australian, Canadian and French infantry and artillery, with massive use of tanks, aircraft and smoke, led to a deep penetration of the German lines, even overrunning divisional headquarters in some places. In the typical pattern of Western Front battles the fighting went on for several days, with the defence gradually reasserting itself over the attack. The General Staff liaison officers sent out to investigate the reasons for the loss of position came back with deeply depressing accounts of the situation.

Six or seven good divisions had simply collapsed under the weight of the British attack. There had been wholesale surrenders; retiring units had denounced reinforcements as 'blacklegs' and 'war-prolongers'. One general said his men handled more like Russian Bolsheviks than German soldiers. Entente casualties had been relatively light; German casualties were severe and a number of divisions badly in need of rest had been drawn into the fighting. Ludendorff was at a loss as to where he was going to get the reinforcements needed to restore the situation and, worst of all, the attackers had captured documents that revealed just how desperate was the German manpower position.

Ludendorff stated quite bluntly for the first time that the war must be ended. He said that 8 August had opened the eyes of the staff on both sides. The Germans could see how weak they were; the Western Allies began to realise that the initiative had passed firmly into their own hands. Hindenburg called a meeting at the Hotel Britannic, Spa, to convey to the chancellor and the secretary of state the bad news. The enemy had not been, and would not be, forced to sue for peace by offensive action. The best that Germany could hope for was to resort to defensive fighting and inflict sufficient casualties on the attackers to make them amenable to diplomatic overtures. Hindenburg was quite optimistic about the situation and the Kaiser, who was drawn into the discussions the next day, even hinted that the field marshal was preparing to court martial the generals who had done so badly on 8 August. The Kaiser is the only source of this story and Admiral Müller wrote it off as one of his 'tall stories'. The Kaiser was surprisingly calm as all this bad news was presented and simply agreed that a way had to be found to end it all as soon as possible. Ludendorff had offered his resignation, suggesting that a fresh pair of eyes might see things more

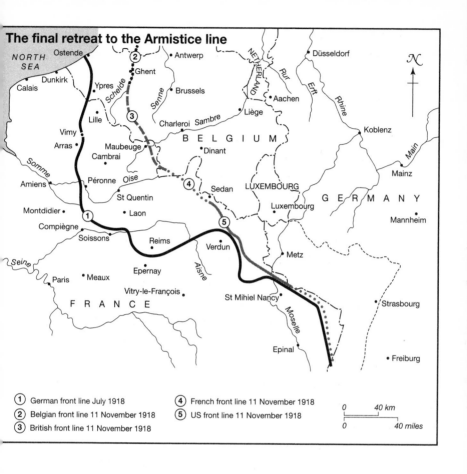

# The final retreat to the Armistice line

**(1)** German front line July 1918
**(2)** Belgian front line 11 November 1918
**(3)** British front line 11 November 1918
**(4)** French front line 11 November 1918
**(5)** US front line 11 November 1918

0   40 km
0   40 miles

clearly. It was too late for that sort of gesture and the offer was refused. Instead Hindenburg endorsed a poster campaign addressed to the German people: 'We have won the war in the East, and we shall win it in the West'. Coming from the beloved national hero, this message was what the people wanted to hear. Such deception would rebound upon its perpetrators when the truth was finally known.

From 21 August onwards came a series of Entente offensives, which developed into a rolling programme of attacks that gave the Germans no respite whatsoever. The British south of Arras, the French along the Oise, then the British north of the Scarpe; the Germans were retreating everywhere, giving up the whole central position between the Somme and the Oise and scuttling out of the Lys salient. As their divisions, unable to replace battle losses and surrenders, shrank dramatically in size, the Germans were falling back to the Siegfried Line and starting new defensive lines in their deep rear all the way back to the borders of the Reich. There was no rest for the infantry and the level of shirking reached epidemic proportions. The desperate combing out of exempted men from Germany was seen as cold comfort, as anyone joining the army from the homeland seemed to bring only discontent and subversion with him.

For the War Ministry to set up a Central Bureau for press and propaganda in August 1918, for which Ludendorff had been asking for years, was too late to be of any influence either at home or abroad. He used this lame effort to redouble his abuse of the German civil government, making it the butt of all his criticism of the authorities that had, according to him, so palpably failed to support the army in its hour of need.

Ludendorff fixated upon the success of British and French tanks in the recent attacks and urgently began a quest for new anti-tank tactics for the field artillery. Even this new attempt at analysis worked against the German Army as now the very appearance of tanks in front of a position became an excuse for the defenders to resume a precipitate retreat.

The news from other fronts – Syria, Palestine, Macedonia and Italy

– was uniformly bad; the Austro-Hungarian Army was crumbling. While Hindenburg continued to be unreasonably optimistic, Ludendorff caused great offence by criticising the fighting capacity of the German troops. Lossberg, the defensive warfare genius who was already doubting the ability of the Siegfried Line to hold for long, remarked acidly that the real fault lay in Ludendorff's defective generalship.

Early in September Ludendorff was showing such obvious signs of nervous strain (temper tantrums, loss of sleep, weeping) that he finally agreed to accept the help of the psychiatrist Dr Hochheimer. He meekly submitted to a new regime of rest, especially of the eyes, of gentle exercise, and of relaxation techniques (even including the singing of folk songs and the contemplation of nature and the beauty of the roses in the garden). There was an immediate improvement in his health, but it was not helped by the news of the first great American effort that saw thirteen divisions of Pershing's First Army crush the St Mihiel salient out of existence.[2]

As he felt better physically and mentally, Ludendorff again became more of an optimist. Yet by the end of September the British and Belgians had begun an offensive that would liberate Belgium once and for all; the main body of the BEF was approaching the Siegfried Line and would smash through it in a single day; the French and Americans were attacking strongly; twenty German divisions on the Western Front had to be disbanded to reinforce others in the line; and then the first of the props of the Quadruple Alliance was kicked away when Bulgaria declared it was seeking a separate peace. There is no doubt that Ludendorff saw this as the last straw. He could envisage the other allies falling away quickly (and they did) and that Germany would be dragged down relentlessly by her numerous enemies.

The generals finally explained to the government just how bad things were, and insisted that Germany must request an immediate armistice. The phrase used repeatedly was that the army was 'at the end of its tether'. It was a terrible shock to the politicians who had never been given the whole truth by the General Staff. It finished the career of Chancellor Hertling. Admiral Müller gave vent in his diary to his feelings about the real culprits:

> But who were our politicians during the war? Hindenburg, Luden-dorff and the political branch of the Great General Staff .... Mistake after mistake had been made, above all the casual handling of peace with Russia, whose collapse had been a boon of immeasurable value to us and should have been exploited to release troops for the West. But instead of this we conquered Latvia and Estonia and became involved with Finland – the results of an excess of megalomania. Very seldom did the actual political leaders manage to prevent the acts of violence planned by the High Command.[3]

It says a great deal about the weakness of German constitutional arrangements that things could have come to such a pass, and explains how the great Western democracies, be they republic or monarchy, had a decided advantage when it came to the conduct of industrialised mass warfare.

On 3 October 1918 Prince Max of Baden (a second cousin of the Kaiser) became Germany's last imperial chancellor. An elderly conservative, of a humanitarian disposition but with no political experience, it is hard to see what he was supposed to achieve. He was immediately assailed by demands from the General Staff for an urgent armistice to stave off the total collapse of the army on the Western Front. Now a delay of forty-eight hours would be a catastrophe. There are reports of staff officers and politicians groaning aloud and sobbing as the real truth was suddenly revealed to them. We can only shake our heads in wonder that such a situation had been allowed to develop. In response to questions from Prince Max, Hindenburg promised that the army could defend the German border until the spring of 1919 (after which their enemies would have overwhelming strength to renew their offensives). Max wondered aloud why Germany didn't just surrender and get it over with.

A note was sent immediately to President Wilson asking him to arrange an armistice based on his Fourteen Points. There is no evidence that either Hindenburg or Ludendorff had actually read Wilson's statement, and they seem unaware of the suggested addendum that called for the destruction of 'arbitrary power' that might disturb the future peace of the world. He was referring to both the Hohenzollern dynasty and the Great General Staff. Having made the first move, the German commanders now seemed to stiffen their resolve to achieve some sort of honourable peace. How crestfallen they were when Wilson's first response was to call for a complete evacuation of occupied territory in the West as a sign of good faith. They clearly thought they were to be given an armistice, a chance to break off the fighting and rest and recover their strength. Hindenburg stated plainly in a letter to his wife:

> The armistice is militarily necessary to us. We shall soon be at the end of our strength. If the peace does not follow, then we have at least disengaged ourselves from the enemy, rested ourselves and won time. Then we shall be more fit to fight than now, if that is necessary. But I don't believe that after two–three months any country will have the desire to begin war again.[4]

It is one thing to be calm in adversity; it is quite another to be so detached from the political reality that was directing the conduct of the war.

It did not help Prince Max that his conciliatory reply to Wilson, offering democratic reform in Germany, coincided with the death by drowning of hundreds of American and British men, women and children in a U-boat attack in the Irish Sea. The fury of the American, French and British people was made manifest in the 14 October demand for Germany to evacuate the occupied territories, end submarine warfare and promise the complete democratisation of Germany (a veiled demand for the Kaiser's abdication).

An indignant Kaiser insisted that the German people rally to their emperor in this hour of crisis; Prince Max finally realised that he had been handed the last word in poisoned chalices. Ludendorff gave a fantastically optimistic review of the military situation, offering to stabilise the front if he could get 600,000 reinforcements and 100,000 replacements a month thereafter. The civil government, with an accession of Social Democrat ministers, had finally learned to treat such reports with a good deal of healthy scepticism.

Hindenburg now insisted that the German Army must fight on to preserve the honour of the nation. It is hard not to see this as a cynical move by the high command to distance the armed forces from the civilians whom they had demanded should seek an armistice. All the while the German divisions on the Western Front were being battered to pieces under the hammer blows of the Western Allies. While key units engaged in a series of fine defensive encounters, there were hundreds of thousands of surrenders by men who had simply had enough. Crown Prince Rupert told the chancellor the true state of the German armies in the West when he wrote that the loss of fuel alone would be absolutely critical within two months.

Wilson's third note (23 October) made it clear that the armistice would be considered as a surrender, that no resumption of hostilities would be permitted at a later date, and that the Allies would only deal with the civil government; the Kaiser must abdicate and the military renounce all power in favour of the civilian leaders. Both Hindenburg and Ludendorff protested separately to Prince Max that this was intolerable and that it threatened the very existence of the country. Crown Prince Rupert simply reminded him that the invasion of Germany itself was imminent and unavoidable.

Clearly not used to the new political realities, Hindenburg and Ludendorff then signed a new official army order to all troops in the field without seeking the approval of the government. That this apparently began life as a press release to the Foreign Ministry that got telephoned to OHL and then written up by a staff officer as an army order adds to the picture of chaos overtaking the German military. Still it went out on 24 October as official policy:

> Wilson's answer is a demand for unconditional surrender. It is thus unacceptable to us soldiers. It proves that our enemy's desire for our destruction, which let loose the war in 1914, still exists undiminished. It proves, further, that our enemies use the phrase 'a just peace' merely to deceive us and break our resistance. Wilson's answer can thus be nothing for us soldiers but a challenge to continue our resistance with all our strength. When our enemies know that no sacrifice will achieve the rupture of the German front, they will be ready for a peace which will make the future of our country safe for the great masses of our people.[5]

This led to one furious row too many in the presence of the Kaiser. Ludendorff was freely abusing the government when the Kaiser took him aside for a severe reprimand for the insubordinate message to the troops and for the way he see-sawed between optimism and pessimism to the consternation of all who looked to him for advice and guidance. The language between the two grew so heated that the Kaiser had to remind 'His Excellency' that he was in the presence of his emperor. Ludendorff went into his by now routine speech about no longer having the Kaiser's confidence and that he was standing in the way of progress. For once the Kaiser took him at his word and accepted his resignation. Hindenburg offered to resign and was ordered to remain at his post. Certainly Ludendorff felt that his old chief was somewhat half-hearted in his bid to quit alongside him and there was bad feeling between them for some time over it. However, it was widely reported that when Ludendorff's departure was announced during 26 October's news bulletins at the cinema audiences burst into spontaneous cheering.

Hindenburg immediately proposed the excellent General Groener as his next chief of staff. Groener was only too glad to leave the thankless task of trying to restore order out of chaos in the Ukraine. He made a fact-finding tour of the Western Front that convinced him that final defeat stared Germany in the face. It was not merely that the divisions of the army were so badly under strength, that rifle battalions were down from seven or eight hundred to two or three hundred men, that no position could be held against the power of their enemy, that men surrendered so freely, and that the losses of guns, mortars and machine guns showed that little effort was being made to get this important heavy equipment away ahead of the retreating infantry. Now both Austria-Hungary and Turkey had asked for armistices to end the fighting on their respective fronts. At home as hunger and influenza sapped the strength of the people, the spectre of Red revolution became a reality. When the German High Seas Fleet at Kiel was ordered out to sea on 4 November on what could only be described as a 'death ride' to meet the Royal Navy, the sailors promptly mutinied, arrested their officers, dampened the ships' boilers and ran up the red flag. When Hindenburg issued an appeal for national unity he was answered by both trade unions and industrialists for a demobilisation office to replace the Imperial Economic Office.

Groener returned to Berlin with an honest and factual report for the chancellor. When Prince Max offered to send an armistice commission to the Entente powers in a week, Groener stated that that was too long and that it must leave the next day. President Wilson had made it clear that the German government would have to apply to Marshal Foch directly to receive the terms of the armistice. On 8 November, as the delegates reached Foch's headquarters, Germany collapsed into a revolutionary situation. Kings, princes and dukes were abdicating; Bavaria declared itself an independent republic; eleven major cities were seized by socialist revolutionaries. Senior army commanders advised the government that their troops could not be relied upon to suppress popular uprisings.

The Kaiser and the Crown Prince, unsafe in Berlin even in the presence of Guards units, were at Spa with OHL. Abdication was openly discussed in both civil and military circles. Both Hindenburg and Groener feared that this would shatter the cohesion of the front-line units. When the Kaiser theatrically considered journeying to the front and 'seeking a soldier's death', Groener would have quite gladly let him go. Hindenburg considered it for a while but decided it was not worth the death of a single German soldier to facilitate such an end. The Kaiser then proposed that he march at the head of his army to put down the rebellion in Berlin. On 9 November Hindenburg and Groener attended the Kaiser for the last time. The field marshal apparently was too overcome with grief and left it to General Groener to tell the Kaiser that he no longer held the confidence of the army or the people. His offer to resign as kaiser but remain as king in Prussia was dismissed out of hand and he knew his fate was sealed.

As the Kaiser abdicated at Spa, Prince Max handed over the chancellorship to the Socialist deputy, Friedrich Ebert, in Berlin. The final act of genius of the German ruling elite was to make sure that none of them were in place to have to accept the harsh but necessary terms of the armistice that came into effect at the eleventh hour of the eleventh day of the eleventh month of the year 1918.

*chapter ten*

# Postscript

Of the two men who effectively led their country to defeat despite contending with a vast array of difficulties, one sank into relative obscurity quite quickly, one rose to be the head of state. Yet their current military reputations are probably the exact reverse of their immediate post-war careers.

For some days after his dismissal Ludendorff sat in a stunned silence at the flat kept by his wife in Berlin. As the civil war developed in the streets outside, bands of Communist sailors and soldiers began chanting his name as a candidate for execution. He was forced to remove, somewhat ignominiously in a heavy disguise, to his brother's house in Potsdam, returning to Berlin on 11 November 1918. He was not safe there and, on being invited to accompany a young captain about to leave for embassy duty in Copenhagen, he, ever the correct soldier, applied to the government for permission to leave Germany. On 16 November, again disguised, he passed through the crowds of revolutionaries in control of all ports and railway stations and escaped to Denmark. As the tide of hate propaganda against him grew, friends in Germany tried to get Hindenburg to speak out publicly in his defence. The field marshal decided that any words from him would be either ignored or counter-productive. Early in December 1918 Ludendorff moved again to Sweden, having turned down a remarkably generous offer from the magnate, Hugo Stinnes, to finance a three-year world tour. His wife would join him by Christmas. Once settled just outside Stockholm Ludendorff began work on his memoirs and, by the end of February 1919, had produced a draft of some 270,000 words – a very productive three month's work. It was written with limited access to official documents and is the work of a consummate staff officer. Understandably it is utterly unapologetic about the actions of the author at all times; the only regrets voiced are that he and his colleagues had not been more demanding of the government and the nation to make greater sacrifices for victory. Certainly the defeat is laid squarely at the door of the government, both imperial and republican. It is a moving tribute to the fighting troops; the book is dedicated 'To the Heroes who Fell Believing in Germany's Greatness'. It was published in two volumes and immediately translated into English and several other languages.

He was able to return to Berlin (using a false name) and was soon being courted by the extreme right in German politics. He produced another two-volume work, *The General Staff and its Problems*, in which he set out documents showing how the German Army was 'held back' before the war, how it had to take on the enormous task of organising the whole nation and its economy for total war, and the General Staff's attitude to the conquered territories and the various peace initiatives.

The imposition of the terms of the Versailles Treaty, backed with the threat of renewed war by the Allied powers in June 1919, led to a new wave of right-wing violence against the detested 'socialist' republican government. By March 1920 the Allied Control Commission had had enough and ordered the disbanding of the worst of the *freikorps*, the volunteer units of ex-soldiers that had bloodily defeated attempts at Communist insurgency in the immediate aftermath of the war. Ludendorff joined the politician, Dr Wolfgang Kapp, in an attempt to overthrow the government. What seemed like an easy success at first was halted by a general strike in Berlin and the subsequent refusal of the military districts outside the capital to support the *putsch*. Kapp fled the country; Ludendorff moved quickly to Bavaria, where he would meet the ambitious Adolf Hitler. He had also abandoned his first wife and taken up with the proto-fascist Mathilde Kemnitz, and his ideas lurched even further to the right. Jews, Freemasons and Catholics joined in one great diabolical conspiracy to explain the disasters that had overtaken Germany. November 1923 was to see him marching at the head of the dismal failure of the Munich *putsch* and the following February saw the humiliation of being the only Nazi supporter on trial to be acquitted. Though an elected Nazi deputy he rarely attended the Reichstag and, after having drifted away from the National Socialists, he allowed himself to be persuaded to stand as their candidate in the presidential elections of 1925. He came bottom of the poll of seven candidates, with 1.1 per cent of the valid votes, and in the second round Hitler swung the party vote behind the narrow victor, Hindenburg. From then on Ludendorff faded into obscurity. He died on 20 December 1937, aged 72, and was given a state funeral by the triumphant Adolf Hitler.

On 10 November 1918, to the great relief of the new civilian government, Hindenburg had announced, through his new First Quartermaster General Groener, 'I will stay on. I won't desert my people in their extremity'.[1] Together they organised the return march of the German field armies. At Cassel Hindenburg was greeted even by the revolutionary soldiery as a national hero. As Germany slid into civil war, with the ultra-left making a bid for power resisted by the state authorities and a plethora of new and extremely bloodthirsty *freikorps*, Hindenburg struggled to uphold the disciplinary record of the army. With OHL relocated to Kolberg, in the heart of old Prussia, he began to get more defiant towards the victors. After a stirring message to the army about preferring death to dishonour in January 1919 he privately advised the government to accept the conditions of the Versailles Treaty.

When the terms were signed on 28 June 1919, he chose that day to resign from the army and issued his last proclamation thanking the troops for their support and loyalty, and hoping that Germany would rise from its present depths of degradation. He retired to Hanover and was warmly received there.

In April 1919 the Reichstag set up a Parliamentary Committee to inquire into the loss of the war. It was empowered to interview any persons who appeared in any way to have been responsible for bringing about, prolonging or losing the war. Four sub-committees would study the treatment of Belgium and war atrocities, violations of the Hague Convention, officer-man relations and the failure to seize opportunities to make peace. This was anathema to the monarchic and military factions and led to a spirited backlash in their political activity. The committee's remit was restricted to the events of 1918 – why the offensives failed, the disorders within the army and the extent to which revolutionary disturbances caused the collapse of the nation. In the event only the first of these topics was ever really investigated.

In November 1919 Ludendorff was called to give evidence and he insisted that Hindenburg be called at the same time. Thus, on 18 November 1919, the two men met for the first time since that fateful 26 October 1918. Together they vigorously defended the position of the Great General Staff in all matters. Reading from a prepared statement, Hindenburg said:

> A general who is not determined to gain the victory for his country must not accept the Supreme Command, unless he receives orders at the same time to capitulate. We had received no such orders. Had we done so, we would have refused to accept the Supreme Command. The Great General Staff was brought up in the doctrines of the great military philosopher, Clausewitz. We look upon war as the continuation of policy by other methods. Our policy of peace was a failure. We didn't want war, and yet the greatest of wars was forced upon us ...

The Chairman interrupted him here, and on several more occasions, to stop voicing overtly political opinion and concentrate on the facts of the matter. The field marshal stolidly continued:

> Whereas in spite of their superiority the various classes and parties in the enemy countries co-operated, and became more and more united in the resolve to win the war, party interests with us gained the upper hand as our position got worse ... Owing to this our will to victory was undermined ... I looked for energy and co-operation but found pusillanimity and weakness.

Hindenburg was building to a 'revelation' that had been carefully imparted to him by Ludendorff:

> Our request for the maintenance of stern discipline and the strict administration of the law was not complied with. Our operations in consequence failed, as they were bound to do, and defeat became inevitable; the revolution was merely the last straw. As an English general very truly said, 'The German Army was stabbed in the back'. There is no need to prove who was responsible.[2]

The army was declaring itself defeated by the revolution in the Homeland and had nothing to blame itself for. Ludendorff then began a tirade against the Socialists and again asserted that their party newspaper had declared it was not in favour of a German victory, though, when pressed, he could never produce the article he regularly referred to. As Ludendorff was roundly abused by the committee some of the old camaraderie revived and Hindenburg intervened to say of his old friend that never would he allow a distinction to be drawn between them. Soon after that they both stormed out of the meeting.

The committee interviewed other important witnesses and published some of their testimonies. Chief among these was General Kuhl, who gave a powerful and well thought out statement of the possibilities in 1918. He thought the balance of forces in 1918 was only marginally in Germany's favour but that the attempt had to be made. He was critical of the lack of strategic guidance from the High Command and greatly regretted how failed attacks were allowed to persist, just in case something might come of them. In summing up the whole effort he wrote:

> Glorious victories were achieved. Great things were accomplished. Many a time we were within an inch of final success. But that inch always failed …. It is doubtful even if all the various diversion attacks had been successful, whether, after the casualties incurred in them, we should have been strong enough for a decisive blow in Flanders.[3]

The great German military historian Hans Delbruck also gave evidence. Later, when Ludendorff had published his memoirs, Delbruck wrote a series of fiercely critical articles, blaming the militarism of the Great General Staff for the defeat. He compares Germany unfavourably to England, where the generals were kept under control by the government. The English understood the dictates of attritional warfare. The German generals wanted nothing less than a victory of annihilation. In staking everything on one last great offensive in 1918 the generals ignored an absolutely vital factor, the dreadful state of German supplies of food and ammunition, and the derelict transportation system servicing their armies. This desperate attempt at a 'Napoleonic' solution to Germany's dire situation threw away the advantages gained in 1917, when a negotiated peace should have been won: 'The German high command had gambled away the war intentionally and criminally and then it had done everything in its power to hinder the start of peace negotiations, asking for them only when it was too late'.[4] In a bitter conclusion, he declared, 'Ludendorff changed the defensive war into a war of conquest. He did not understand the strategic requirements of the war and, by his resistance to the king and government, brought on the revolution that finally buried the German Empire'.[5]

By March 1920 Hindenburg had completed his own war memoirs

(*Out of My Life*) in which his simplicity and modesty were apparent. He repeated the 'stab in the back' theory in flowing classical language: 'Our worn-out front collapsed as Siegfried did beneath the spear thrust of the treacherous Hagen'.[6] He did manage to infuriate Ludendorff all over again by revealing the moment of indecision at Tannenberg on 26 August when Ludendorff fleetingly considered breaking off the battle, and only Hindenburg's calm and placid nature held everything together.

It was Tirpitz who persuaded Hindenburg to stand in the 1925 presidential elections as a sort of national unity candidate, and he won (if only by the narrow margin of 14.6 million votes to 13.7 million). As we might expect he accepted the verdict as a duty to be performed for the nation. He steered his fractious country through a series of critical issues with the occupying powers and gradually saw a return of prosperity and respectability. In 1927 a huge monument was opened on the site of the victory of Tannenberg. Ludendorff was there but, after a brief handshake, showed no sign of wanting to be reconciled to his old chief. Hindenburg's speech repudiated the 'war guilt' clauses of the Versailles Treaty and repeated the mantra of the German Army: 'It was not envy, hate or desire for conquest that made us draw the sword .... With clean hearts we marched out to defend the Fatherland, and with clean hands did we wield the sword'.[7]

In 1928, without his consent, the Right campaigned on the slogans 'Down with the November Criminals!' and 'Extend the Powers of the President'. They went down to a crushing electoral defeat at the hands of the Socialists and Communists. Hindenburg maintained his steady and calming influence in the country, despite being increasingly denounced as a 'renegade' by the Right, and at the age of 84 was re-elected president in 1932, beating the rising Hitler in both rounds of the ballot. As political crises mounted in a Germany badly hit by the international recession that followed the Wall Street Crash, Hindenburg was finally, if reluctantly, obliged to invite Adolf Hitler to become the chancellor of Germany in 1933. Mercifully Hindenburg died soon after, in August 1934, before he saw too much more of the depths to which his beloved country could sink under her new leadership.

These two men, Hindenburg and Ludendorff, sum up in a remarkably precise way the history of early twentieth-century Germany. One was a perfect representative of the cash-poor Junker class that was the very embodiment of the union between the Prussian king and his army that created first the nation and then the empire. The other was a commoner whose innate talents were recognised by that army that was a state within a state and was a perfect representative of that Pan-German drive of militarists, industrialists and financiers that would come to see their king-emperor as an increasing irrelevance.

Having established a glorious military reputation in 1914, saving East Prussia from 'the Cossacks' at a time when everything was going wrong in the West, they endured a period of frustration while Falkenhayn carried out his grand strategy of adjusting to the very kind of attrition warfare that Germany was least able to cope with in the long run. When they were called to supreme command in 1916 it was to take over a military situation that was anything but optimistic. The losses on the Western Front, through the fighting at Verdun and on the Somme, were thought of as the death of the old army. In the East, Germany was 'shackled to a corpse' as Austria-Hungary neared her breaking point under the Brusilov offensives. At home the shortages caused by the failure to plan for a long war, and by the increasing grip of the naval blockade, were sapping the will of the nation to resist.

Together these two men made a thorough and realistic assessment of the situation. In the West they sanctioned a withdrawal from hard-fought territory to stronger defensive positions and inaugurated a new phase of doctrine and training in the armies in the field. They withstood a punishing series of offensives by the Entente powers that nearly broke the French Army for good, and which inflicted grievous losses on a British Expeditionary Force that was developing its offensive capacity to a most deadly and alarming degree. In the East they were able to crush the newly engaged Romanian enemy swiftly and exploited the chaos in Russia after the fall of the tsar to put one of their major opponents out of the war once and for all. At home they threw the weight of the experts of the Great General Staff behind a massive programme to mobilise the German economy for total war, and the organisation of the nation's manpower and morale for a last great effort. They ruthlessly engaged in domestic politics to force out government ministers in whom they had no confidence and replaced them with ciphers who would do the bidding of the 'silent dictatorship' that they had become.

The skilled use of Germany's small strategic reserve gave a spec-tacular victory over Italy that gave another huge boost to the national will to continue a war that was making life at home an increasing misery. In one huge gamble they gave the authority of the army to the attempt by the navy's submarine fleet to destroy Great Britain's ability to continue the war by a campaign of unrestricted sinking of shipping entering and leaving her ports. After some stunning early successes, and the rise of a deep pessimism in the ruling circles of Great Britain, it was realised quite quickly that the gamble had failed and had, instead, made an official belligerent of the United States of America that had been the unofficial arsenal of the Entente for so long.

The success against Russia and Italy gave a new air of confidence to the military–industrial complex supporting the army in its struggle to force a peace with advantage upon the Entente. The German Army and people responded with one last gasp of enthusiasm to the prospect of a final great assault to settle matters on the Western Front. Once again the formidable duo completely reorientated the dominant posture of the German armies in the field and organised and trained them in the new attack doctrines.

The attack launched in March 1918 had a primary objective to defeat the BEF and drive it back in ruins against the Channel ports.

France would not survive the defeat of its principal ally, and it would all be over before the Americans could deploy an army of any consequence. The sheer violence of the German onslaught led to dramatic early success and hope of victory must have soared. But the British Army just would not collapse as expected and the French came to their aid with unexpected vigour. After two offensives failed a series of diversionary attacks against the French were made, always with the aim of returning to settle accounts with the British in Flanders. The end result was a million casualties Germany could not afford and a new front line that would be very difficult to defend once the Western Allies resumed the initiative. Through all this travail, they could not resist trying to develop a new German empire in the East that fatally drained away military assets that should have been concentrated for the main effort.

The attempt to achieve complete victory had failed and the truth that broke over the German people and their government came as a terrible shock. The remarkable German soldier continued to fight with courage and skill but was relentlessly driven back towards the borders of Germany by battle-hardened veterans of the British, French and Belgian armies, aided by rapidly growing numbers of Americans. Relying on the proven defensive excellence of their soldiers, they tried to keep resistance going for far longer than was reasonably sensible. Their nation collapsed into civil war and their emperor was forced to flee the country.

In all accounts of the war from the German side the name of Ludendorff dominates that of Hindenburg. The German military system allowed for the chief staff officer to have enormous powers of direction of military resources and operations, whilst nominally under the command of a senior figure. The system made the commander-in-chief ultimately responsible for success or failure, but the work was done by the like-minded professionals schooled by the thoroughly scientific military machine that was the Prussian/German Army, the evolution of which was described in Chapter One. Ludendorff thrived on work, lots of work, and he saw his task as embracing the whole military, economic and social organisation of Germany and its conquered territories to bring about the final victory. He had no faith in the civilian government of Germany, itself the product of a poorly developed democracy, to carry the nation forward in an effective manner. It was, of course, too much for one man, regardless of the number of excellent staff officers around him. He felt everything relating to the success of his mission very deeply and, when under stress, became of a very nervous disposition, subject to violent mood swings. The more sympathetic of subsequent biographies of him would carry titles such as *Tormented Warrior* or *Tragedy of a Specialist*.

What this driven man needed was the massive, steady and calming influence of Field Marshal Hindenburg, to give him the freedom to develop his ideas, to reassure him at times of crisis and to take final responsibility for what were always joint plans and decisions. It is true that, as the war progressed, Hindenburg was increasingly marginalised by the frenetically active coterie around Ludendorff, and earlier admirers like Groener came to see Ludendorff as a 'two-faced rogue' and Hindenburg as little more than his front man. The military historian and critic, Basil Liddell Hart, once famously described France's Marshal Joffre as a 'national sedative'.[8] Hindenburg was important to the German people as a symbol that, while he was at the helm, all would be well in the end.

Together these men guided the armed forces of Germany against a sea of enemies that inexorably grew in number, regardless of German victories against them. After ending the year 1917 in as good a strategic position as any in the war, they staked everything on a final offensive in 1918 and, because they would not or could not concentrate on one issue at a time, led their nation to defeat. The extraordinary development of civil-military relations in Germany had as much to do with that defeat as anything any two soldiers could accomplish.

Great commanders can lead their countries to calamitous defeat.

One has only to think of Hannibal and Napoleon, whose reputations survive regardless of their final acts. One could add Robert E. Lee to that pantheon, and remember that Frederick the Great only survived complete annihilation in the field by the timely death of the sovereign of one of his most implacable enemies. To properly assess greatness, one needs to consider the circumstances in which high office was attained, the overall situation faced, in both the short and long term, and the subsequent handling of the resources and instruments of war available to maximum advantage. All these factors have to be taken into account as we arrive at our own private judgements on Field Marshal Paul von Beneckendorff und von Hindenburg and General Erich Ludendorff.

# Bibliography

Place of publication is London unless otherwise stated.

Asprey, Robert, *German High Command at War: Hindenburg and Ludendorff and the First World War* (Little, Brown, 1991)

Barnett, Correlli, *The Swordbearers: Studies in Supreme Command in the First World War* (Penguin, 1966)

Dupuy, Col. T. N., *A Genius for War: The German Army and General Staff 1807–1945* (Hero Books Virginia, 1984)

Falkenhayn, General von, *General Headquarters 1914–1916 and Its Critical Decisions* (Hutchinson, 1919)

Feldman, G. D., *Army, Industry and Labour in Germany, 1914–1918* (Berg, 1992)

Fischer, Fritz, *War of Illusions: German Policies, 1911–14* (Chatto & Windus, 1975)

Goldsmith, M. & Voigt, F. A., *Hindenburg: Man and Legend* (Faber, 1930)

Goodspeed, D. J., *Ludendorff: Soldier, Dictator, Revolutionary* (Rupert Hart-Davis, 1966)

Herwig, Holger, *The First World War: Germany and Austria-Hungary 1914–18* Hodder Arnold, 1997)

Hindenburg, Field Marshal Paul von, *Out of My Life* (Cassell, 1920)

Hunt, D. (ed.), *War Aims and Strategic Policy in the Great War* (Croom Helm, 1977)

Ironside, Maj. Gen. Sir E., *Tannenberg: The First Thirty Days in East Prussia* (Blackwood, 1925)

Kennedy, Paul (ed.), *War Plans of the Great Powers, 1880–1914* (Allen & Unwin, 1985)

Kitchen, Martin, *Silent Dictatorship* (Croom Helm, 1976)

Ludendorff, General Erich, *The General Staff and its Problems* 2 vols. (Hutchinson, 1920)

Ludendorff, General Erich, *My War Memories 1914–1918* 2 vols. (Hutchinson, 1919)

Ludwig, Emil, *Hindenburg and the Saga of the German Revolution* (Heinemann, 1935)

Macksey, Kenneth, *Why the Germans Lose at War: The Myth of German Military Superiority* (Greenhill, 1996)

Moyer, L. K., *Victory Must Be Ours: Germany in the Great War, 1914–1918* (Leo Cooper, 1995)

Nevin, Thomas, *Ernst Junger and Germany: Into the Abyss, 1914–1945* (Constable, 1997)

Parkinson, Roger, *Tormented Warrior: Ludendorff and the Supreme Command* (Hodder & Stoughton, 1978)

Ritter, R., *The Schlieffen Plan* (Wolff, 1958)

Rutherford, W., *The Tsar's War, 1914–1917* (Faulkner, 1992)

Schultze-Pfaelzer, Gerhard, *Hindenburg: Peace-War-Aftermath* (Philip Allen, 1931)

Showalter, Dennis, *Tannenberg: Clash of Empires* (Archon USA, 1991)

Stein, General von, *A War Minister and his Work* (Skeffington, n.d.)

Stone, Norman, *The Eastern Front, 1914–1917* (Scribners, 1975)

Tschuppik, Karl, *Ludendorff: Tragedy of a Specialist* (Allen & Unwin, 1932)

Wheeler-Bennett, J. W., *Brest-Litovsk* (Macmillan, 1966)

Wheeler-Bennett, J. W., *Hindenburg: The Wooden Titan* (Macmillan, 1967)

William of Germany, Crown Prince, *My War Experiences* (Hurst & Blackett, n.d.)

Zabecki, D., *Steel Wind: Colonel Georg Bruchmüller and the Birth of Modern Artillery* (Praeger, 1994)

# Notes

## CHAPTER ONE

1 Dupuy, Trevor, *A Genius for War: The German Army and General Staff 1807–1945* (Hero Books, USA 1984) p. 48

2 ibid. p. 116

## CHAPTER TWO

1 Ludwig, Emil, *Hindenburg and the Saga of the German Revolution* (Heinemann, 1935) p. 20

2 ibid. p. 29

3 Schultze-Pfaelzer, Gerhard, *Hindenburg: Peace-War-Aftermath* (Philip Allen, 1931) p. 52

4 ibid. p. 60

5 Ludwig, Emil, op. cit. p. 35

6 Goldsmith, Margaret & Voigt, Frederick, *Hindenburg: Man and Legend* (Faber, 1930) p. 66

7 Ludendorff, General Erich, *My War Memories 1914–1918* (Hutchinson, 1919) Vol. I, p. 25

8 Wheeler-Bennett, John, *Hindenburg: The Wooden Titan* (Macmillan, 1967) p. 8, f/n. 1

9 Ludendorff, General, op. cit. vol. I, pp. 31–2

10 ibid. p. 41

11 ibid. pp. 42–3

## CHAPTER THREE

1 Parkinson, Roger, *Tormented Warrior: Ludendorff and the Supreme Command* (Hodder & Stoughton,1978) p. 50

2 ibid. p. 55

## CHAPTER FOUR

1 Müller, Admiral Georg von, *The Kaiser and His Court* (Macdonald, 1961) p. 187

2 ibid. Entry for 30 July 1916

3 Ludendorff, General Erich *My War Memories 1914–1918* (Hutchinson, 1919) vol. I, p. 239

## CHAPTER FIVE

1 Ludendorff, General Erich *My War Memories 1914–1918* (Hutchinson, 1919) vol I, p.270

2 ibid. p. 272

3 William of Germany, Crown Prince *My War Experiences* (Hurst & Blackett, n.d.) pp. 239–240

4 By contrast the British Army, after it had commissioned everyone possible from the universities and professions, promoted large numbers of men from the ranks to 'Temporary Commissions'. On the armistice in 1918 this category formed a majority of officers in the BEF.

5 Ludendorff, General Erich op. cit., vol. I, p.386

6 Ludendorff, General Erich *My War Memories 1914–1918* (Hutchinson, 1919) vol I, p.387

7 It should come as no surprise that the BEF, sharing a common experience with the German Army, was also producing large numbers of training pamphlets based on lessons learned from the fighting, and that many of its staff officers at all levels were former regimental officers with a good understanding of the realities of war at the front.

8 Quoted in Asprey, Robert, *The German High Command at War* (Little Brown, 1991) p. 265

9 Ludendorff, General, op. cit. p. 240

10 ibid. p. 242

11 Ludendorff, General Erich, op. cit. pp. 339–40

12 Müller, Admiral Georg von, *The Kaiser and His Court* (Macdonald, 1961) p. 204

## CHAPTER SIX

1 See Lee, John, 'The British Infantry in 1917: Some Lessons of the Somme' in *Look to Your Front: Studies in the First World War* (Spellmount, 1999), a collection of essays by members of the British Commission for Military History

2 Ludendorff, General Erich, *My War Memories 1914–1918* (Hutchinson 1919) vol. II, p. 421

3 Kitchen, Martin, *Silent Dictatorship* (Croom Helm, 1976) p. 94

4 Ludendorff, General, op. cit. vol. I, p. 335

5 Ludendorff, General, op .cit. vol. II, p. 450

6 Ludendorff, General, op. cit. vol. II, p. 451

7 Kitchen, Martin op. cit. p. 134

8 Ludendorff, General, op. cit. vol. II, pp 460–61

9 Ludendorff, General, op. cit. vol. II, p. 476

10 Ludendorff, General, op. cit. vol. II, p. 488

11 Müller, Admiral Georg von. *The Kaiser and his Court* (Macdonald, 1961)

12 Ludendorff, General, op. cit. vol. II, pp. 489–90

13 Ludendorff, General, op. cit. vol. II, pp. 490–1

14 Ludendorff, General, op. cit. vol. II, p. 491

15 Ludendorff, General, op. cit. vol. II, p. 502

16 Ludendorff, General, op. cit. vol. II, p. 511

## CHAPTER SEVEN

1 Kitchen, Martin, *Silent Dictatorship* (Croom Helm, 1976) p. 165

2 Ludendorff, General Erich, *My War Memories 1914–18* (Hutchinson, 1919) Vol. II, p. 549

3 Müller, Admiral Georg von, *The Kaiser and his Court* (Macdonald, 1961) p.

4 Kitchen, Martin, op cit. p.

## CHAPTER EIGHT

1 Edmonds, Brig. Gen. James, *British Official History: Military Operations, France and Flanders 1918* vol. I, p.140

2 In the 1815 campaign against Napoleon this was said when the entire Saxon corps in Flanders deserted Prussian service and it had to be shipped home.

3 Ludendorff, General Erich *My War Memories 1914–1918* (Hutchinson, 1919) vol. II, pp. 587–8

4 ibid. pp. 600–601

5 ibid. p. 614

6 ibid. p. 647

7 ibid. p. 640

**CHAPTER NINE**

1 Ludendorff, General Erich, *My War Memories 1914–1918* (Hutchinson, 1919) vol. II, p. 679

2 This 'American' victory was supported by four French colonial divisions; most of the 3,200 guns were French, with 1,500 French and British aircraft and 250 French light tanks.

3 Müller, Admiral Georg von, *The Kaiser and his Court* (Macdonald, 1961) entry for 29 September 1918

4 Asprey, Robert *The German High Command at War* (Little, Brown, 1991) p. 473

5 ibid. p. 482

**CHAPTER TEN POSTSCRIPT**

1 Schultze-Pfaelzer, Gerhard, *Hindenburg: Peace-War-Aftermath* (Philip Allen, 1931) p. 175

2 ibid. pp. 201–2

3 *The German Offensives of 1918: The Record of General von Kuhl*, RUSI Journal, February 1928

4 '*Ludendorff's Self-Portrait*' (1922) in Delbruck's *Modern Military History*, (Nebraska University Press, 1997) p. 192

5 ibid. p. 192

6 Schultze-Pfaelzer, G., op. cit. p. 211

7 ibid. p. 313

8 Liddell Hart, Basil, R*eputations: Ten Years After* (Little, Brown, 1928)

# Index